C L A S S I C
Linens II

SYMBOL OF EXCELLENCE PUBLISHERS, INC.

Dedication

This book is lovingly dedicated to my husband Wayne and our sons, Eric and Brian. Each day with you brings all the fun and happiness one could ever hope to have.

Phyllis

For Jim, Catherine, Mitchell, and Emily— You give me great joy and make my life complete.

Barbara

Contents

TABLECLOTHS 4
   Garland of Fruits 6
   Blue Silhouette 8
   Pansy Parade 10
   Happy Birthday 12
   Grape Arbor 14
   Wedding Bells 16
   Celebrations 18
   Wildflower Garden 20
TABLE RUNNERS 22
   Magnolia Blossom 24
   Grandma Hill's Bouquet 26
   Bountiful Harvest 28
   Primitive Table Runner 30
   Reindeer And Ribbon 32
   Parasol Bouquet 34
PLACE MATS 36
   Four Flowers On Navy 38
   Rose Trellis 40
   Nursery Rhyme Border 42
   Jingle Bells 43
   Forget-Me-Nots And Ribbons 44
   Three Letter Monogram Collection 46
   Monogram Quartet 48
   Fruits And Berries 50
THE CARE OF LINENS 55
GENERAL INSTRUCTIONS AND
HELPFUL HINTS 56
CHARTS 59
   Garland of Fruits 59

Blue Silhouette 62
Pansy Parade 65
Happy Birthday 68
Grape Arbor 75
Wedding Bells 79
Celebrations 83
Magnolia Blossom 87
Grandma Hill's Bouquet 89
Reindeer And Ribbon 92
Bountiful Harvest 93
Primitive Table Runner 95
Parasol Bouquet 97
Four Flowers On Navy 99
Rose Trellis 104
Forget-Me-Nots And Ribbons 105
Jingle Bells 106
Nursery Rhyme Border 107
Three Letter Monogram Collection 110
Monogram Quartet 115
Wildflower Garden 118
Fruits And Berries 123
SHOPPERS GUIDE 127
CREDITS 128

The finishing instructions and yardage for finishing materials have been written and calculated for the projects shown, stitched on the fabric listed for each project in its color code. Alternate fabric choices have also been listed. If you wish to stitch a design on an alternate fabric, or alter the placement of a design or repeating design, you will need to re-calculate the finished size of the project, as well as the yardage of finishing materials needed, and make necessary dimension adjustments when finishing.

Tablecloths

GARLAND OF FRUITS
BLUE SILHOUETTE
PANSY PARADE
HAPPY BIRTHDAY
GRAPE ARBOR
WEDDING BELLS
CELEBRATIONS
WILDFLOWER GARDEN

The pleasure of meals shared, whether a party in the true sense or simply a gathering of one's immediate family members, can be enhanced when the mood is set by elegant table linens. Enjoyment of gathering for a meal can be the highlight of a busy day.

We have assembled a collection of tablecloths which are equally at home on formal tables in separate dining rooms, on informal tables in a kitchen, or covering a table set up on a patio or in a garden. Three of the tablecloths included in this chapter were selected because the stitchery adorning them can be tied to special celebrations in our lives—birthdays, weddings, and anniversaries. We suggest making a tradition of using these cloths for family events, and perhaps sharing them with special friends for their personal celebrations.

To insure that your pleasure in the stitched tablecloth is complete, please note a few precautions. Before stitching the design, make sure the fabric is properly sized for the use you have selected. Choose finishing materials, such as lace edging and insertion trim, with the same care exercised in selecting the ground fabric for the tablecloth. Remember to select trims which are similar in weight and feel to the fabric you have chosen.

Use heavy linen cloths over a silence pad or a blanket to soften sound and anchor the cloth in place. Cloths using lace insertion should be used over a bare table to allow the wood to show through, or over an undercloth in a color which enhances the overall look of the stitched piece.

Use your stitched tablecloth with pride—it's a work of art!

GARLAND OF FRUITS

Nature's sweet gift, lush fruits in a riot of color, translates into a border which can be easily adapted for any table—round, oval, or rectangular. Reminiscent of the popular Della Robbia wreaths, this realistic swag of fruits can be stitched end to end to form a circle, or placed side by side to create an oval, scalloped effect. Stitched in a circle, the design perfectly frames a punch bowl, making this cloth an excellent choice for use at receptions and teas.

BLUE SILHOUETTE

A garden table set for a luncheon party for six creates a perfect backdrop for displaying your collection of assorted blue dishes. Antique patterns and new china pieces mix comfortably on a cloth stitched using one pattern segment. You can easily extend this silhouette design, stitched in one shade of dark blue, to fit a tablecloth of any length, or the simple square overcloth shown here. If you are the proud owner of an extensive, or growing, collection of this popular collectible china, these place mats will also be a "must have" set for you. Using this pattern which complements the *Blue Silhouette* tablecloth, simply stitch the band down the side of the place mats, and add a motif and simple border to matching napkins.

PANSY PARADE

Show off your stitchery with a square tablecloth that is too pretty to hide under serving dishes. Two designs, stitched twice, and placed together patchwork style with lace inserts, create the center section of this cloth. Use it alone, or over a floor length table skirt, and expect compliments! A matching bread cover can also be made, using the design which complements the tablecloth.

HAPPY BIRTHDAY

Grandfather's birthday is sure to be a special occasion when his grandchildren are on hand to share in the celebration. The festive table is spread with a birthday tablecloth designed to be used for all the family birthdays—from the oldest member to the youngest. Stitched in bright colors, the center floral design provides the perfect spot for placing the birthday cake, and tiny candles "marching" around the border will delight the youngsters in your family.

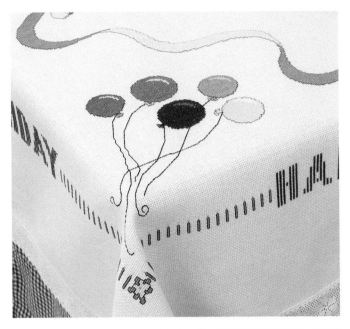

GRAPE ARBOR

Whether you choose to use this lovely piece as a table topper, or as an afghan, *Grape Arbor* will soon become a favorite personal touch in your home. True-to-life colors are used to add luscious grape clusters to a length of Louisiana afghan fabric. This captivating design proves again the versatility of both needlework and decorative accent pieces.

WEDDING BELLS

When the bride and groom cut the wedding cake, make sure the photographer captures this elegant tablecloth, stitched for the occasion. Worked in softest pastels and silvery highlights, the ribbons and bells corner motif adds a touch of the unexpected to a festive celebration. The cloth is perfect for use at bridal teas and anniversary celebrations as well.

CELEBRATIONS

The table is ready for an anniversary dinner for two and it promises to be a sentimental, memory-making occasion. The candles are lit, and a gift package waits on the plate. The evening will be a special celebration of the year past and the future yet to be shared. Let the memories be enhanced by the anniversary cloth you have stitched for just such an occasion. Consider establishing a family tradition by loaning the cloth to family members and special friends for use on their own anniversary dates.

WILDFLOWER GARDEN

Bring a sampling of the beauty of nature's flowers indoors to enjoy all year round when you stitch this elegant afghan which can double as a small table cover. Floss colors were chosen to duplicate nature's own palette. If you are feeling especially generous with your time, you might consider presenting this marvelous piece to a special friend at gift-giving time.

Table Runners

MAGNOLIA BLOSSOM
GRANDMA HILL'S BOUQUET
BOUNTIFUL HARVEST
PRIMITIVE TABLE RUNNER
REINDEER AND RIBBON
PARASOL BOUQUET

Marvelous lengths of elegant fabric, embellished with fine stitchery, can be an important part of your household's linen collection. Table runners serve many purposes, with the most important being, perhaps, that of adding to the room's decor. In addition, runners provide protection for that portion of the table where a centerpiece and candlesticks are placed.

You may choose to use table runners on the dining room table between formal dinners, or you may elect to leave the decorative runner and simply add plain place mats and napkins to dress the table for dinner.

The designs presented in this chapter can all be used in your home in several ways—from the traditional tabletop position, to gracing a foyer table, or protecting a bedroom dresser top. The versatile designs range from the magnificent magnolia blossom to a quick-to-stitch primitive design.

Create a collection of wonderful cross stitched runners for your home and use them as they suit your mood!

MAGNOLIA BLOSSOM

Bring the grace and charm of the Old South into your home with this lavishly detailed magnolia blossom. Stitched to enhance a table runner used on a foyer table, or a runner given a place of honor at your next formal dinner party, this design will continue to please you as the years pass.

GRANDMA HILL'S BOUQUET

Based on the design found on one of her 1930s dresser scarves, *Grandma Hill's Bouquet* re-kindles memories of gathering with cousins at Grandma's house for weekend spend-the-night parties, posing in front of the mirror, with powder boxes and hair brushes atop the dresser scarf, and sinking into deep feather beds when Grandma called for lights out. Used here as a runner to grace the table for afternoon tea, this design would be equally at home, as it was then, on a dresser scarf. Choose pastel colors, or antique pastel colors, for stitching this design.

BOUNTIFUL HARVEST

Thanksgiving, that special celebration born in thankful Puritan hearts in the seventeenth century, is often characterized for us by a filled-to-overflowing cornucopia, such as this stitched tribute. The use of this masterful work of art in stitches can become one of your holiday traditions, along with turkey, cranberry sauce, and pumpkin pie. Or use this table runner year-round to symbolize the goodness of God and the blessings of a productive earth.

PRIMITIVE TABLE RUNNER

Capture a bit of Americana in stitches with this informal cloth which is equally at home inside an early American house or on the porch of a log cabin. Part of its country charm is its versatility since it can be used as a table runner, a dresser scarf, or a table topper wherever you choose to use it. The pleasure you'll receive from both the stitching of the piece and the displaying of your finished work accounts for the rest of its charm.

REINDEER AND RIBBON

Holidays provide the best of reasons for calling together family and friends. Whether the focus of your entertaining is a formal seated dinner or a festive dessert party, you can set the stage with this quickly stitched table runner embellished with a single color ribbon and reindeer design. If holiday red doesn't fit your color scheme, simply choose another fabric, or choose a floss color to suit your home and stitch the silhouette design on white fabric.

PARASOL BOUQUET

The charm of Great-Grandmother's Victorian bedroom comes to life on this decidedly feminine dresser top. Protecting the wood surface and providing a resting place for important necessities is the purpose of this charming scarf, a reminder of days gone by. Re-create a bit of that early era with this piece, which was custom hemstitched using a Bernina sewing machine.

Place Mats

FOUR FLOWERS ON NAVY
ROSE TRELLIS
NURSERY RHYME BORDER
JINGLE BELLS
FORGET-ME-NOTS AND RIBBONS
THREE LETTER MONOGRAM COLLECTION
MONOGRAM QUARTET
FRUITS AND BERRIES

Add imagination to mealtimes through your creative use of place mats you have custom stitched for your home. Changing the mood of the dining area, whether it is a bay window nook off the kitchen, or the more formal dining room table, is as simple as selecting a set of place mats.

Place mats show off the beauty of a wood table and serve to define place settings. They provide protection while adding a softening touch to the table's surface.

If your time for stitching is limited, or you don't have the inclination to start a large tablecloth, place mats are a perfect choice for your stitchery moments.

Interest in personalized linens is increasing, so we have chosen several simple designs for inclusion in this chapter. Although we show some designs stitched on place mats and another style stitched on bath linens, all the designs in this chapter can be used on your choice of linens. While one's initials could be used alone, we like the addition of color provided by the circle of flowers and the shield design. Using waste canvas allows you to stitch these designs even on the thickest terry towels!

The custom of personalizing linens, from table linens to bath and bed linens, can be traced to earlier centuries when linens were rotated for even wear. Some stitchers used an intricate lettering and numbering system to keep track of their linens. While this practice is no longer necessary, using a monogram adds a certain touch of elegance to otherwise plain linens.

There is more flexibility today in the styling of monograms, although the large center initial should be the first letter of the last name. If you are stitching a gift for a bridal couple, you can stitch the bride's married initials, or you can use the husband's first initial to the left of the center letter, with the wife's first initial balancing the monogram on the right. For stitching the shield monogram series, use the initials that you favor.

FOUR FLOWERS ON NAVY

Ideal for lunch on the terrace, this quartet of stitched beauties from nature will provide the perfect beginning to a table set for casual elegance. Stitched on navy fabric, these designs will lend enjoyment to the last lazy days of summer, and capture a slice of its charm for you to enjoy the whole year through.

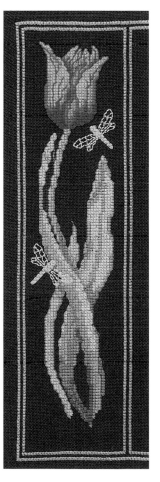

ROSE TRELLIS

An intimate luncheon for two on the patio is a perfect time to bring out this pair of place mats heavily stitched with diagonal diamonds and bordered with English chintz in a popular cabbage rose pattern. Pink Lazy Daisy stitches at the intersecting lines add a delicate touch of color, which is repeated in the plates.

NURSERY RHYME BORDER

Delight your favorite youngster with a place mat made especially for him. Nursery rhyme highlights and snippets of words parade around the edges of this clever mat, which will surely make mealtime more interesting for a member of the younger set. Start a tradition of using classic table linens when your child is young, and he'll have an appreciation for elegant tables all his life.

JINGLE BELLS

Add a special touch to your holiday table with these inspired-by-the-season designs. Used on place mats and napkins which will surely garner praise from your yuletide guests, these quick to finish designs can also be stitched on a variety of other pieces that will be perfect for gift-giving at this special time of the year.

FORGET-ME-NOTS AND RIBBONS

When you invite a special friend for lunch, add interest to your dining table with simple fringed place mats and matching napkins enhanced by a stitched shaded bow, surrounded by tiny flowers. These lovely sets have two advantages: they are easy to stitch and they are made from easy-care fabric.

THREE LETTER
MONOGRAM COLLECTION

Alphabet letters, in three shapes, mix and match perfectly to allow you to personalize with ease your bath linens, pillowcases, dresser scarves, or table linens. These versatile letters were charted to work in any combination, and using waste canvas on non-even-weave fabrics means you can place your monogram anywhere!

MONOGRAM QUARTET

Adding your personal stamp to a dinner party is as simple as stitching your monogram on table linens made for just such special occasions. Whether it's a formal gathering, or a more casual get-together, your guests are sure to marvel at your decorative table. Choose a dainty floral motif, or a more formal shield design, and let the floss colors used in the stitching dictate napkin colors. For special family gatherings, you might consider stitching each family member's initials on his or her own place mat.

FRUITS AND BERRIES

Brighten a breakfast table with place mats sporting colorful clusters of rich, ripe berries, realistically created in stitches. Select one favorite pattern and repeat it to stitch a matching set of place mats, or stitch one of each design for a vivid assortment of fruits from vines.

RASPBERRIES

BLUEBERRIES

BLACKBERRIES

STRAWBERRIES

FRUITS AND BERRIES

Tea time is a perfect time for using these charming mats, edged in lace and embellished with perfect, lush fruits. Whether you choose casual fringed place mats, or more elegant lace trimmed ones, you'll enjoy both stitching and using these sets.

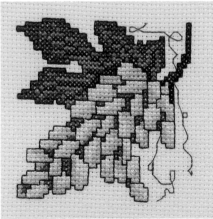

GRAPES

WATERMELON

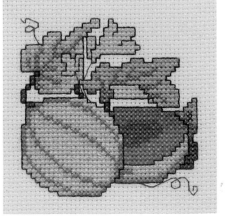

CANTALOUPE

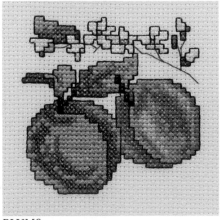

PLUMS

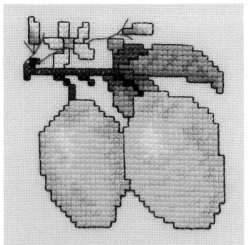

LEMONS

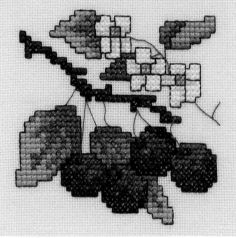

CHERRIES

FRUITS AND BERRIES

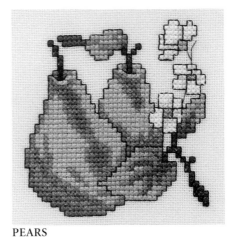

PEARS

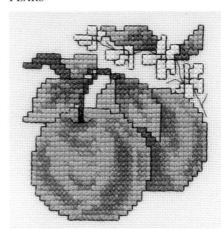

ORANGES

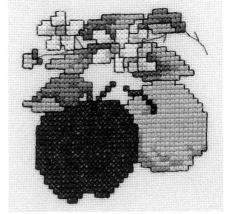

APPLES

The assortment of *Fruits and Berries* designs takes on added versatility when worked in the corners of a tablecloth. Whether you prefer to work this colorful stitchery on a pre-finished piece, or you choose to make your own tablecloth using scrap fabric, you're sure to treasure these additions to your collection of table linens.

PEACHES

THE CARE OF LINENS

Fine linens deserve the best possible care. Proper care also enhances the look of your table linens and assures their long life.

The most desirable way to store linens is flat, un-ironed, and unfolded. While a china cabinet or hutch drawer will provide adequate space for storing place mats and small accessory linens, full-sized cloths, such as those required by a truly formal dinner, will require another method of storage.

For larger linen cloths, a method of rolling for storage is recommended. A cardboard tube, a minimum of one inch in diameter, should be covered with a clean white fabric or acid-free tissue paper. The cloths can then be rolled gently around the tube and covered with more white fabric or acid-free tissue.

If it is not possible to roll larger table linens, they may be gently folded and stored where no other item is placed atop the linen. Never press in creases or folds. Linen thread is very durable, but it also tends to be brittle, so creases and folds increase the possibility of thread breaking or cracking.

Caution should be exercised in selecting a location for storing linens. Avoid exposure to excessive heat or dampness. Do not place linens in plastic or airtight bags. Linen is a natural fiber and should be allowed to breathe.

Table linens made of cotton or synthetic fabrics can be washed, dried, and pressed with the same care afforded today's fine fabrics. Items made of linen fabric should be gently washed by hand in mild soapy water and rinsed thoroughly. Remove as much water as possible by gently pressing the cloth between large thick terry towels. **DO NOT WRING.** Drape over two or three clotheslines. Do not pin. Pinning the cloth to the line will result in distortion of the thread lines. If a clothesline is not available, cover a shower curtain rod with thick towels and drape the cloth over it.

Do not use bleach on linen pieces. Use other standard stain removal practices.

When linens are thoroughly dry, store un-ironed. Press just before using. Steam pressing adds moisture to the fibers, and if linens are stored after such pressing, mildew could result.

GENERAL INSTRUCTIONS AND HELPFUL HINTS

PREPARATION

Before stitching the design, "bleed" individual skeins of identical floss colors by rinsing them in a solution of one tablespoon white vinegar and eight ounces clear water. Rinsing in this method should release any excess dye. Follow with a water rinse, and continue this process until water remains clear. Then blot floss, and lay it aside to dry, being careful to keep it from tangling. **DO NOT WRING.** When stitching on colored ground cloth, it is best to pre-wash the cloth in mild soapy water to set the color, rinsing it thoroughly, allowing it to dry, and blocking it prior to stitching. White and ivory ground cloths need not be washed for colorfastness prior to stitching, but may be pre-washed if desired. If not washed before stitching, pieces should be washed and blocked before attaching the lace or trim.

Pre-shrink all insertion and edging lace before attaching it to the fabric.

PROPER CUTTING TECHNIQUES

There is a proper way to cut even-weave fabrics. To insure proper length and width, the fabric must be cut on the grain.

As shown in the photographs (right), linen is cut by pulling a thread, then cutting in the "track" left by the removed thread.

The other even-weave fabrics (Aida, Hardanger, etc.) have a grain, or "track", that is easy to see for cutting guides.

Whatever fabric is selected, the straight edge is important for fringing, hemming, or attaching trim. (Refer to "General Finishing Instructions".)

PROPER CENTERING TECHNIQUE

The placement of the design on a large piece of fabric can be tricky. These simple steps make centering easy.

Fold the fabric lengthwise to find the center. As shown (page 57), place a long center running stitch the entire length of the cloth.

Fold the fabric to find the center of the width. Place a long running stitch on the center line. The

two basting threads will cross in the center of the cloth. This will provide five reference points for stitching. Leave basting threads in until piece is finished. (You will use the center mark when measuring to the edges of the fabric for finishing.)

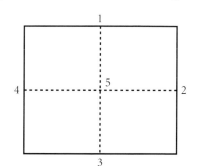

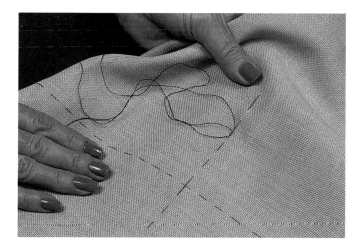

PLAN A PROPER FIT FOR YOUR TABLECLOTHS

The illustrations given here show standard tablecloth sizes for rectangular, oval, and round tables. If you are fortunate enough to own an antique dining table, check carefully to determine the proper size needed for your special cross stitched cloths. Most tables built in more recent years will be covered by the following illustrations.

To determine the size your cloth should be, measure the width and length of your table. For formal cloths, add 20 inches to both dimensions to allow for a 10-inch drop on all sides. For less formal cloths, smaller drops of 6-8 inches on all sides are acceptable. For a 6-inch drop, add 12 inches to both dimensions.

For an 8-inch drop, add 16 inches to both dimensions. Consider the number of people to be seated at the table. If you add a leaf or leaves to your table, be sure your guiding measurements reflect those additions. A proper fitting cross stitched cloth will be a gift of yourself for today and for the future.

Standard Tablecloth Sizes

52 x 70 Rectangle	52 x 70 Oval	60-inch Round
60 x 84 Rectangle	60 x 84 Oval	68-inch Round
60 x 92 Rectangle	60 x 92 Oval	70-inch Round
60 x 104 Rectangle	60 x 104 Oval	

PROPER PIECING TECHNIQUES

Many of the even-weave fabrics used for tablecloths are not wide enough to cover the tabletop plus the overhang on all sides. When the fabric is not wide enough, additional fabric is added to the sides, as illustrated.

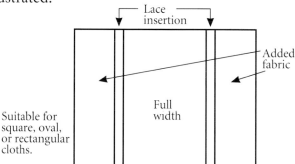

Round cloths may also require piecing. When they do, the additional fabric is added before the fabric is cut into the round shape.

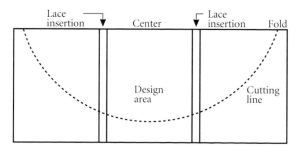

NEVER PIECE FABRIC IN THE AREA WHERE THE DESIGN IS TO BE STITCHED.

GENERAL FINISHING INSTRUCTIONS

To achieve an even finish on all sides of a stitched piece, measure out from the center of the fabric and mark the desired finished edge. By following the "tracks" of even-weave fabric, or creating them to follow on linen, you can be sure to achieve straight lines to follow when finishing your cross stitched pieces.

When hemming, turn raw edges under once and press. Turn under again, using hem width desired, stitch around perimeter of piece, and press.

When applying lace, a narrow hem, such as a shirttail hem of ¼", works well for finishing raw edges. Simply hem the piece first, and apply lace trim to edge of piece atop hem, mitering at the corners.

When fringing, mark desired finished size of piece. Determine desired fringe width and mark. (This marking will be inside that made for the finished piece.) At marking for finished size, trim edges even, pulling threads if necessary to create a "track" for cutting. At inside marking, machine stitch along "track", pulling threads if necessary to create one. Fringe by pulling threads from edges to machine stitching.

FINISHING TABLECLOTHS

There are a number of ways to finish tablecloths, ranging from simple hemmed edges to lace application and inserts to drawn work. Of course there is no one best way. The design and the fabric it is stitched on, as well as the intended use of the cloth and the personal taste of the owner, affects the way the piece will be finished.

Specific finishing instructions have been given for the tablecloths presented in this book. Those instructions appear on the applicable chart pages, along with the color codes and stitching instructions.

FINISHING ACCESSORY TABLE LINENS

Most of the place mats, napkins, breadcovers, and table runners presented in this book were stitched on pre-finished items. If you wish to make these items from scratch, following is a list of standard dimensions, and general information.

Standard Accessory Table Linens Sizes

Place mats	13" x 18"
Napkins	15" x 15"
Breadcovers	18" x 18"
Table Runners	(The size of the runner will be determined by the size of your table, and whether you wish to place the runner horizontally or vertically on the table.)

When making accessory table linens from scratch, cut fabric approximately 2" larger on all sides than finished size desired. This will give you ample fabric for making edges even and finishing as desired. Finish following the instructions listed in "General Finishing Instructions".

FINISHING DRESSER SCARVES

The size of the dresser or other piece of furniture on which the scarf is to be used will dictate the size of the scarf. To determine desired finished size, measure top surface of dresser, and determine how much of dresser you wish scarf to cover. In addition, if you wish to let the scarf hang over the edges of the dresser, you will need to make that adjustment when calculating the length.

As with accessory table linens, cut fabric 2" larger on all sides than finished size desired.

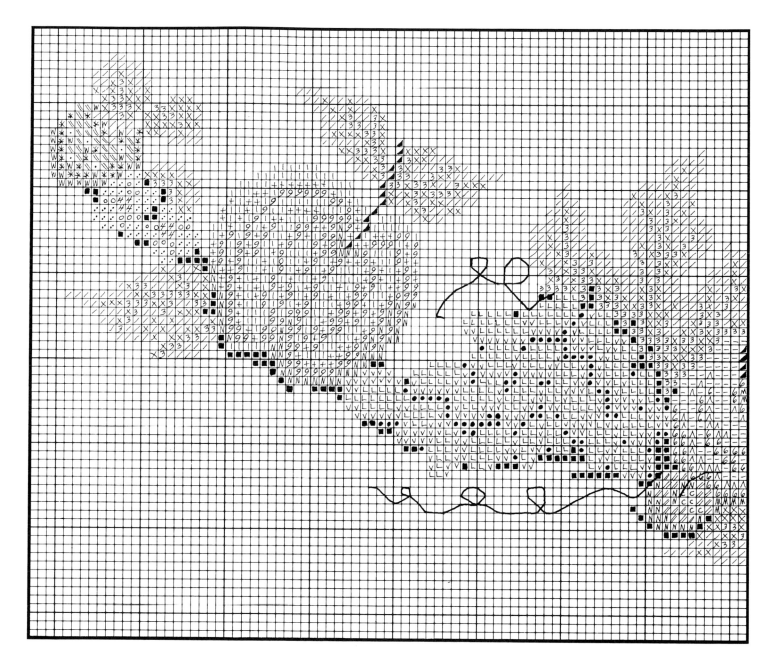

GARLAND OF FRUITS TABLECLOTH

DMC	Coats	Anchor®	
N	814	3044	44 garnet, dk.
9	815	3000	22 garnet, med.
+	498	3410	43 red, dk.
I	304	3401	19 red, med. (two skeins)
●	550	4107	102 violet, vy. dk.
V	552	4092	101 violet, dk.
L	553	4097	98 violet, med. (two skeins)
	554	4104	96 violet, lt.
z	720	—	326 spice, dk.
	223	3241	895 pink, med.
	721	—	324 spice, med.
=	721	—	324 spice, med.
	223	3241	859 pink, med.
	722	—	323 spice, lt.

\	722	—	323 spice, lt.
	725	2298	305 topaz
	223	3241	859 pink, med.
//	815	3000	22 garnet, med.
	223	3241	859 pink, med.
c	223	3241	859 pink, med. (two skeins)
M	720	—	326 spice, dk.
6	721	—	324 spice, med.
	741	2314	314 tangerine, med. (two skeins)
∧	722	—	323 spice, lt.
	741	2314	314 tangerine, med.
-	741	2314	314 tangerine, med.
w	817	2335	19 coral red, vy. dk.
*	349	2335	13 coral, dk.
↘	351	3011	10 coral
•	353	3006	8 peach flesh
·•	white	1001	01 white

4	741	2314	314 tangerine, med.
	725	2298	305 topaz
o	762	8510	397 pearl gray, vy. lt.
■	934	6270	862 avocado-black (two skeins)
3	937	6268	268 avocado, med. (three skeins)
x	470	6010	267 avocado, lt. (four skeins)
/	471	6010	266 avocado, vy. lt. (four skeins)
◢	3021	5395	273 brown-gray, dk.
bs	3012	—	844 khaki, med.

Fabric used for model: 25-count cream Dublin linen from Zweigart®
Stitch count: 68H x 241W (one panel only)
Complete design: 27 ½" diameter
Approximate design size:
    25-count—19 ¼" x 5 ½" (one panel only)

Shaded portion indicates overlap from previous page.

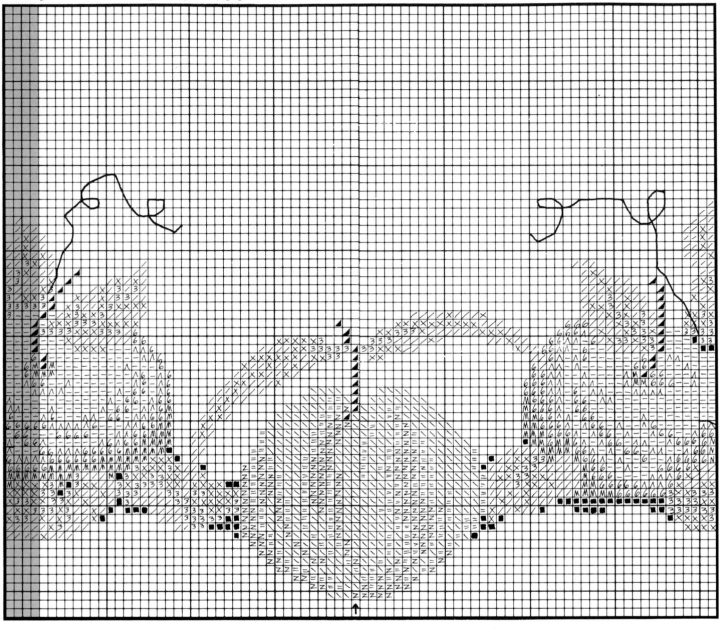

Instructions: Cross stitch over two threads using three strands of floss. Backstitch using two strands of floss. When two colors are bracketed together, use two strands of first color and one strand of second color. When three colors are bracketed together, use one strand each.

Backstitch (bs) instructions:

| 3012 | — | 844 | grape tendrils |
| 3021 | 5395 | 273 | cherry stems |

Special instructions:
(Square tablecloth)
1. For square cloth shown, purchase a 45" x 45" piece of fabric, 5 ½ yds. complementary lace of your choice, and matching thread.
2. Find center of tablecloth, and begin stitching

top of peach stem 11" from center of fabric, and four threads to the left of center. To achieve circular pattern, repeat entire design four times, overlapping strawberries. **Where the pattern meets, stitch the strawberry only once.**
3. To finish, make a narrow hem around edges, and attach lace atop hem, mitering at corners.
(Oval or rectangular tablecloth)
NOTE: Instructions given are for linen.
1. Determine desired size for tablecloth, and purchase needed fabric, trim, and thread.
2. Find the center of the tablecloth, and begin stitching top of peach stem 11" from center of fabric, and four threads to the left of center. Leave one space (two threads) between the strawberries and stitch design side by side. Repeat design as

many times as necessary, forming a garland, to fill side of tablecloth. Complete stitching on one side of cloth first. Then stitch **both** ends before beginning second side. **NOTE:** If you wish to alter the placement of the side garland, you will need to re-calculate the measurements for placement, keeping in mind the number of times the complete design will fit across the ends of the tablecloth on which you are stitching.
3. To turn the corners, do not repeat the strawberry. Simply overlap as on the square cloth (circular design).
4. Finish as desired.

Designed by Cathy Livingston

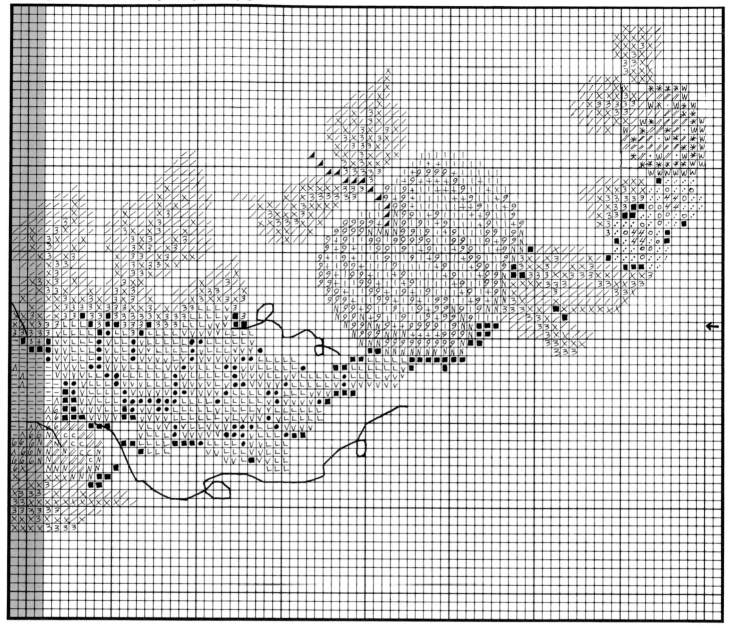

61

BLUE SILHOUETTE TABLECLOTH

DMC Coats Anchor®
● 820   7024   134   royal blue, vy. dk.

Fabric used for model: 25-count white Lugana®
from Zweigart®
Stitch count: 58H x 165W (one panel)
Approximate design size:
    25-count—4 ⅝" x 13 ¼"
    28-count—4 ⅛" x 11 ¾"
    30-count—3 ⅞" x 11"
    32-count—3 ⅝" x 10 ¼"

NOTE: Set floss color before beginning, referring
to "General Instructions and Helpful Hints."
Instructions: Cross stitch over two threads using
three strands of floss. Backstitch using two strands
820/7024/134.
Finishing instructions:
1. Purchase 49" x 49" piece of fabric, 6 yds.
complementary lace, and matching thread.
2. For square tablecloth shown, measure in 3"
from one corner and begin stitching. Repeat design as indicated in Illustration A, turning cloth as
you stitch. Note that in the corners the designs do
not overlap, but stack (see ill. A).

3. To finish, make a shirttail hem around perimeter of tablecloth and attach lace over hem,
mitering at corners.
NOTE: For a rectangular tablecloth, the design
may be repeated indefinitely. (See ill. B for design
placement.) Add side panels for desired length.
You may wish to use lace inserts between tablecloth
and panels.

Designed by Dot Young

Shaded portion indicates overlap from previous page.

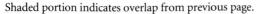

Illustration A

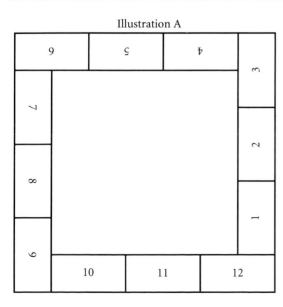

Flower motif in far right corner is shown to indicate placement of design if repeated end to end, as for a rectangular or oval tablecloth. Flower motif at the top center shows placement of design on a square cloth, such as the one photographed.

Illustration B

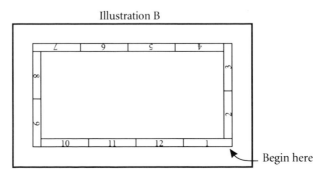

BLUE SILHOUETTE PLACE MAT

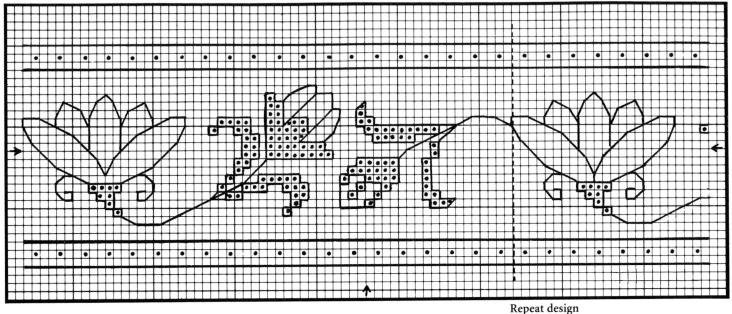

Repeat design

BLUE SILHOUETTE PLACE MATS AND NAPKINS

DMC Coats Anchor®
● 820 7024 134 royal blue, vy. dk.

Fabric used for model: 26-count white Sal-Em cloth pre-finished place mats and napkins with lace from Carolina Cross Stitch, Inc.
Stitch count:
    Place mat 60H x 27W (one panel)
    Napkin 42H x 36W
Approximate design size:
Place mat
    26-count—4 ⅝" x 2"
Napkin
    26-count—3 ¼" x 2 ¾"
NOTE: Set floss color before beginning, referring to "General Instructions and Helpful Hints."
Instructions: Cross stitch over two threads using three strands of floss. Backstitch using two strands 820/7024/134. Center design vertically on place mat and begin stitching in center of design from the left side of the place mat. Repeat design in both directions until reaching upper and lower edges of place mat. NOTE: We stitched the design so that the large flowers open toward the center of the place mat. Stitch napkin design 1" in from left edge and 1" up from lower edge, placing flower in lower left-hand corner of napkin.

Designed by Dot Young

BLUE SILHOUETTE NAPKIN

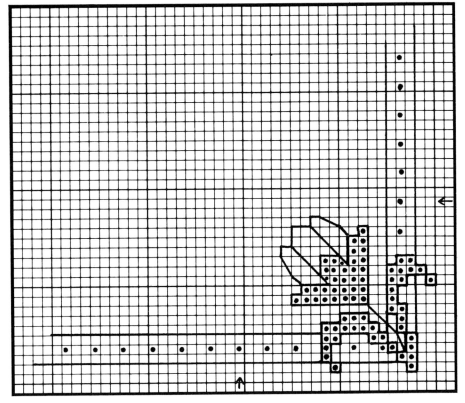

64

PANSY PARADE TABLECLOTH

	DMC	Coats	Anchor®	
■	310	8403	403	black
*	333	—	119	blue-violet, dk.
3	3746	—	—	blue-violet
V	340	7110	118	blue-violet, med.
−	341	7005	117	blue-violet, lt.
◢	3371	5478	382	black-brown
w	920	3337	339	copper, med.
+	720	—	326	spice, dk.
=	740	2099	316	tangerine
/	741	2314	314	tangerine, med.
•	white	1001	01	white
‖	3727	—	969	mauve
c	316	3081	969	mauve, med.
x	315	3082	972	mauve, dk.
❾	902	3083	897	garnet,
▲[	550	4107	102	violet, vy. dk.
[	902	3083	897	garnet, vy. dk.
N[	327	4101	100	violet, dk.
[	552	4092	101	violet, dk.
⌐	553	4097	98	violet, med.
\	554	4104	96	violet, lt.
❙	3078	2292	292	golden yellow, vy. lt.
o	727	2289	293	topaz, vy. lt.
⫽	725	2298	305	topaz
z[	433	5471	944	brown, med.
[	3371	5478	382	black-brown
✗	471	6010	266	avocado, vy. lt.
●	890	6021	212	pistachio, ul. dk.
6	319	6246	246	pistachio, vy. dk.
>	367	6018	210	pistachio, dk.
◣	791	7024	178	cornflower, vy. dk.
M	792	7150	177	cornflower, dk.
L	793	—	176	cornflower, med.
bs	415	8510	398	pearl gray

Large Pansies Left and Right
Fabric used for model: 27-count off white linen from Norden Crafts
Stitch count: 86H x 86W
Approximate design size:
    14-count—6 ⅛" x 6 ⅛"
    18-count—4 ¾" x 4 ¾"
    27-count—6 ⅜" x 6 ⅜"
    32-count—5 ⅜" x 5 ⅜"

Instructions: Cross stitch over two threads using two strands of floss. Backstitch using one strand of floss. Straight stitch stems by ribbons using one strand 890/6021/212. When two colors are bracketed together, use one strand of each.
NOTE: Cut four squares of fabric, each 13" x 13". Center design on each square of fabric. Stitch each design twice.
Backstitch (bs) instructions:
    890   6021   212 stems within bouquet
    415   8510   398 white areas on pansies
Finishing instructions:
1. Complete all stitching following instructions given.
2. Purchase 12 ½ yds. of 2 ½"-wide lace to match fabric. (Lace with a straight finished edge on both

sides is preferable.)
3. Hem raw edges of each square to prevent fraying. To form main section of tablecloth, place each of the four squares so that the bouquet points toward the center. (Refer to illustration.) Fit lace between squares, overlapping at the center, and stitch along edges to attach to tablelcoth. To complete main section, attach lace around perimeter of tablecloth, mitering at corners.
4. When main section is completed, cut two linen panels (A), each approximately 12" x 31". NOTE: Panel A must be the exact length of main section. Adjust if needed.
5. Attach one panel A to top side and one to bottom side of main section, using a ½" seam allowance, and referring to illustration for placement.
6. Cut two linen panels (B), each approximately 12" x 60". NOTE: Panel B must be the the exact length of main section plus both top and bottom panels A. Adjust if needed.
7. Attach one panel B to each side of tablecloth, using a ½" seam allowance, and referring to illustration for placement.
8. Zigzag raw edges separately and press seams open.
9. To complete, attach lace around perimeter, mitering at corners.

Pansy Bread Cover

Fabric used for model: 27-count off white linen from Norden Crafts
Stitch count: 40H x 40H
Approximate design size:
    14-count—2 ⅞" x 2 ⅞"
    18-count—2 ¼" x 2 ¼"
    27-count—3" x 3"
    32-count—2 ½" x 2 ½"

Instructions: Cross stitch over two threads using two strands of floss. Backstitch using one strand 3371/5478/382. Straight stitch for stems below leaves using one strand 890/6021/212.
NOTE: Cut fabric 17" x 17". Stitch design in lower right corner, 1" in from side and 1" up from lower edge of fabric.
Finishing instructions:
1. Purchase 1 ⅛ yds. 1"-wide, complementary lace of your choice for each piece you wish to make.
2. Hem raw edges of fabric to prevent fraying.
3. Attach lace around perimeter of fabric, mitering at corners.

Designed by Cathy Livingston

BREAD COVER

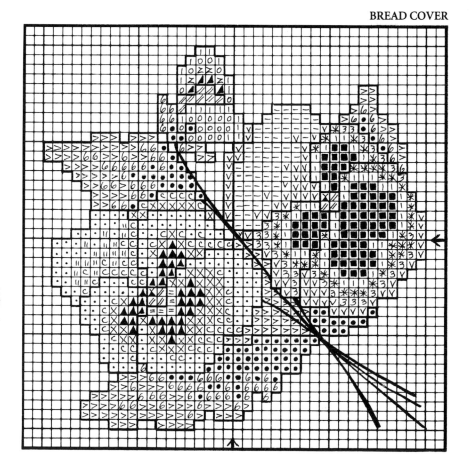

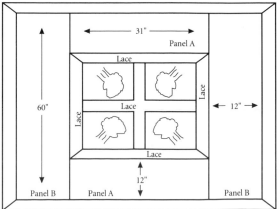

HAPPY BIRTHDAY TABLECLOTH

DMC	Coats	Anchor®	
• 747	7053	928	sky blue, vy. lt.
s 519	—	168	sky blue
∕ 518	—	169	wedgewood, lt.
x 517	7162	170	wedgewood, med.
ℓ 3348	6266	264	yellow-green, lt.
o 906	6256	256	parrot green, med.
bs 367	6018	210	pistachio green, dk.
● 666	3046	46	red, bt.
3 3689	3086	49	mauve, lt.
c 3687	3088	68	mauve
6 351	3011	10	coral
·· 307	2290	289	lemon
9 746	—	275	off white
− 743	2302	302	yellow, med.
★ 970	2327	316	pumpkin, lt.

8 208	4301	111	lavender, vy. dk.
V 211	4303	342	lavender, lt.
+ 869	—	906	hazelnut, vy. dk.
bs 3371	5478	382	black-brown

Fabric used for model: 14-count white Aida
Stitch count: 460H x 460W
Approximate design size:
    14-count—33" x 33"
    18-count—26" x 26"

NOTE: Begin stitching at center of tablecloth, 10" in from bottom edge, referring to schematic for placement. Complete Sections 1-6 on lower half of tablecloth first. Then turn your cloth 180° to finish second half. Repeat Sections 1-6, referring to schematic for placement.
Instructions: Cross stitch using two strands of floss. Backstitch using two strands of floss unless indicated otherwise.
Backstitch (bs) instructions:

367	6018	210	stems of flowers
3371	5478	382	strings on balloons, remainder of backstitching (one strand)

NOTE: When backstitching candle, be sure to stitch the wick (between symbols ▬ and ╲).
Finishing instructions:
1. Purchase 45" x 45" piece of fabric, 5 ½ yds. complementary lace, and matching thread.
2. Complete all cross stitch following instructions given.
3. To finish, make a shirttail hem around perimeter of tablecloth, and attach lace over hem, mitering at corners.

Designed by Dot Young

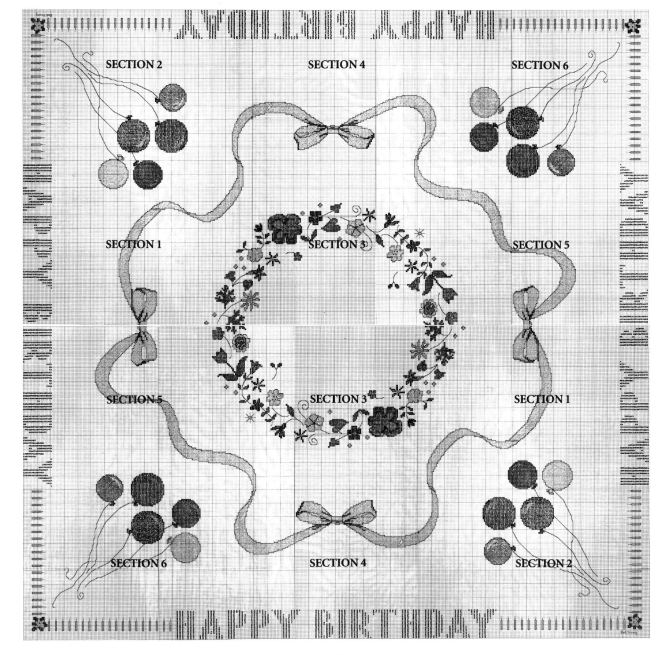

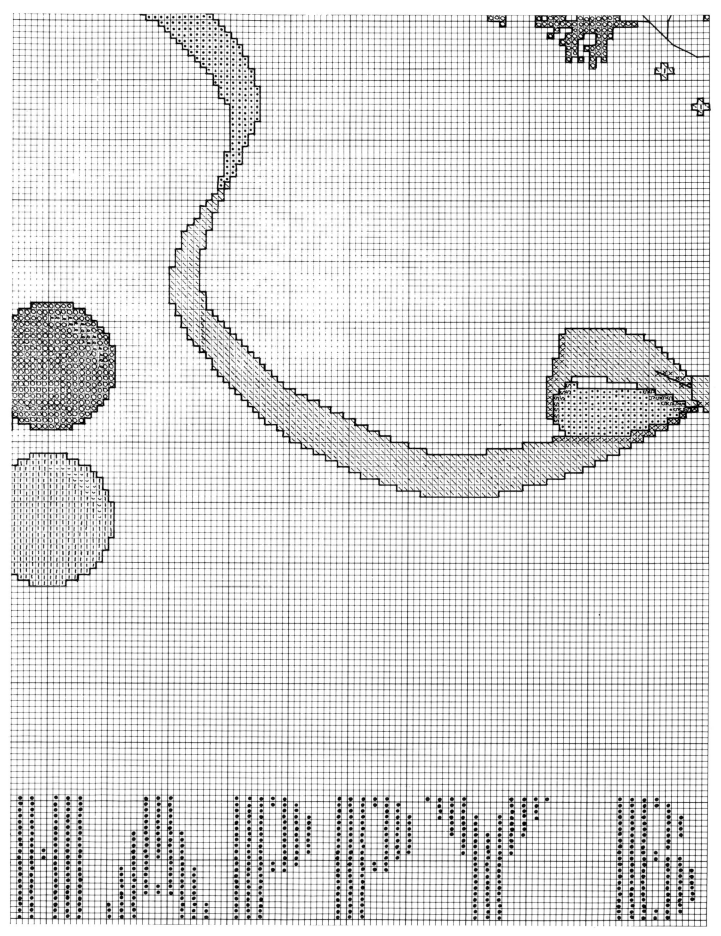

TOP

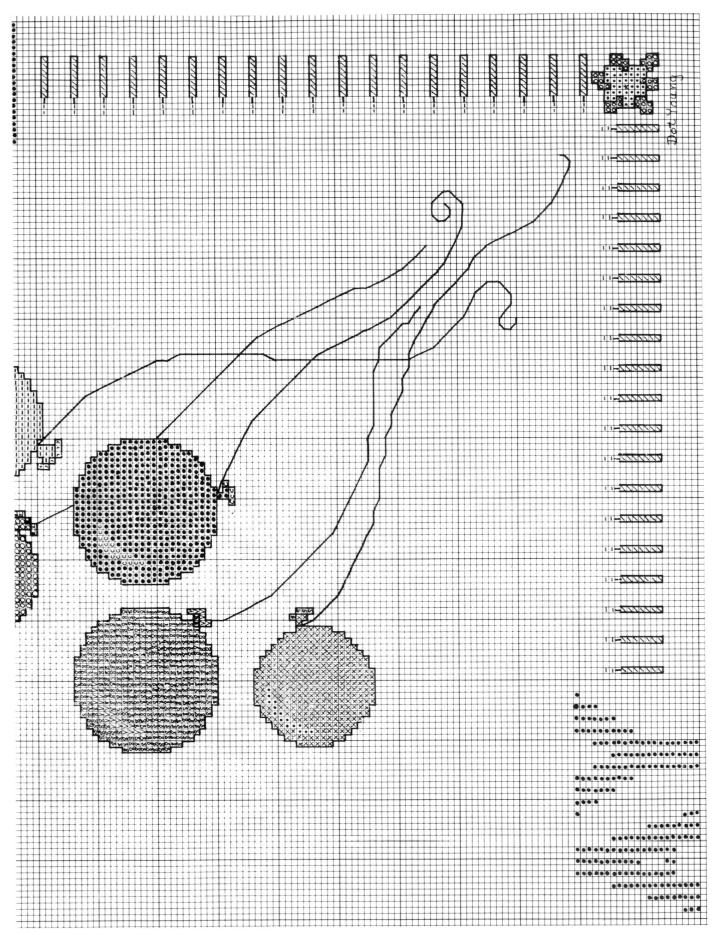

TOP

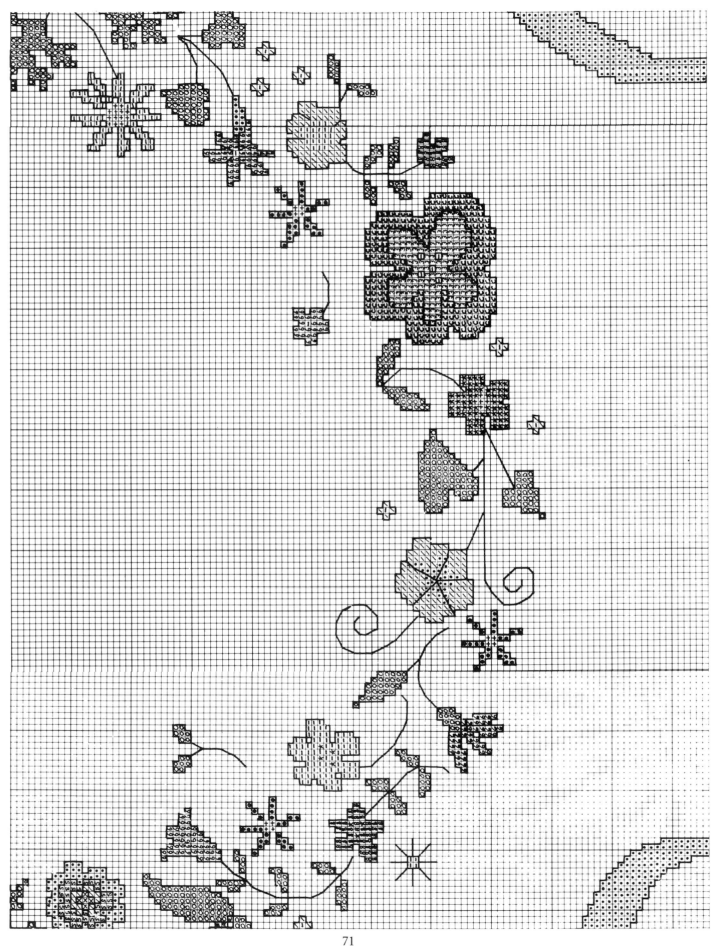

TOP

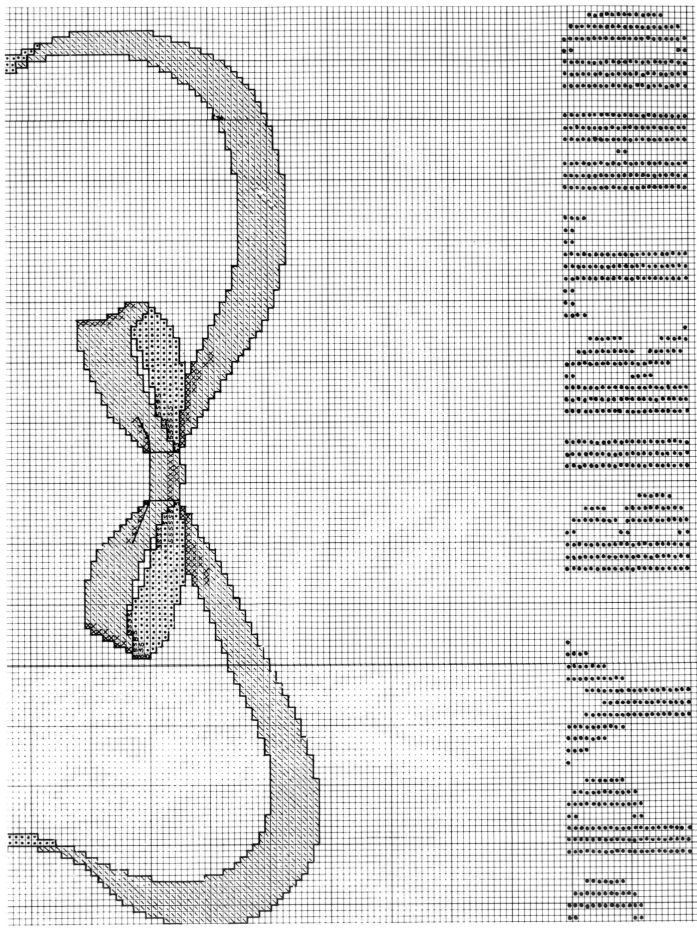

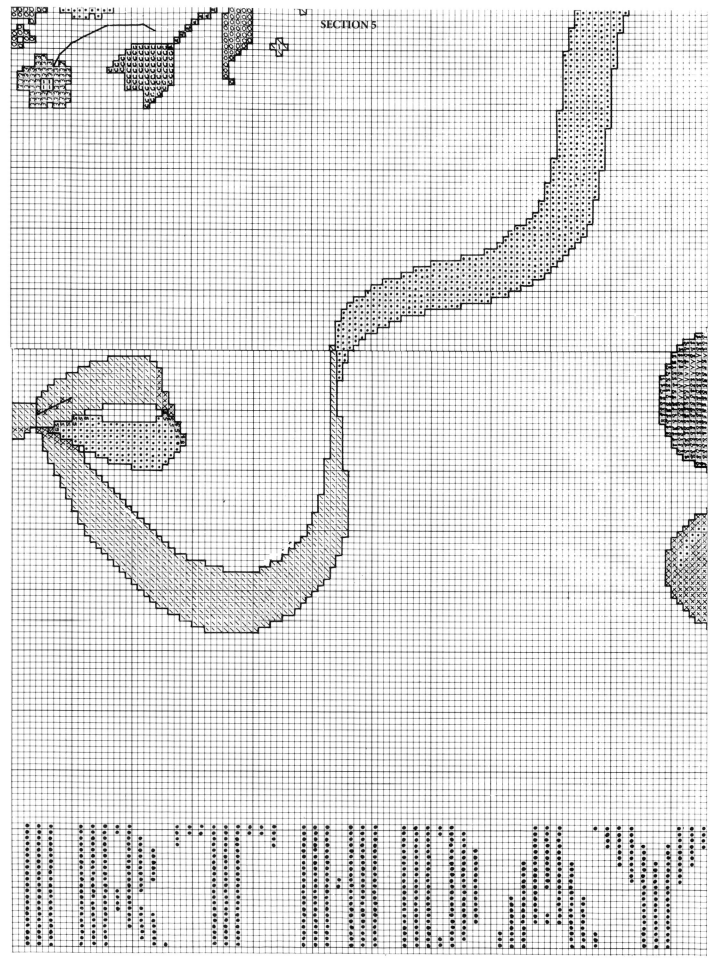

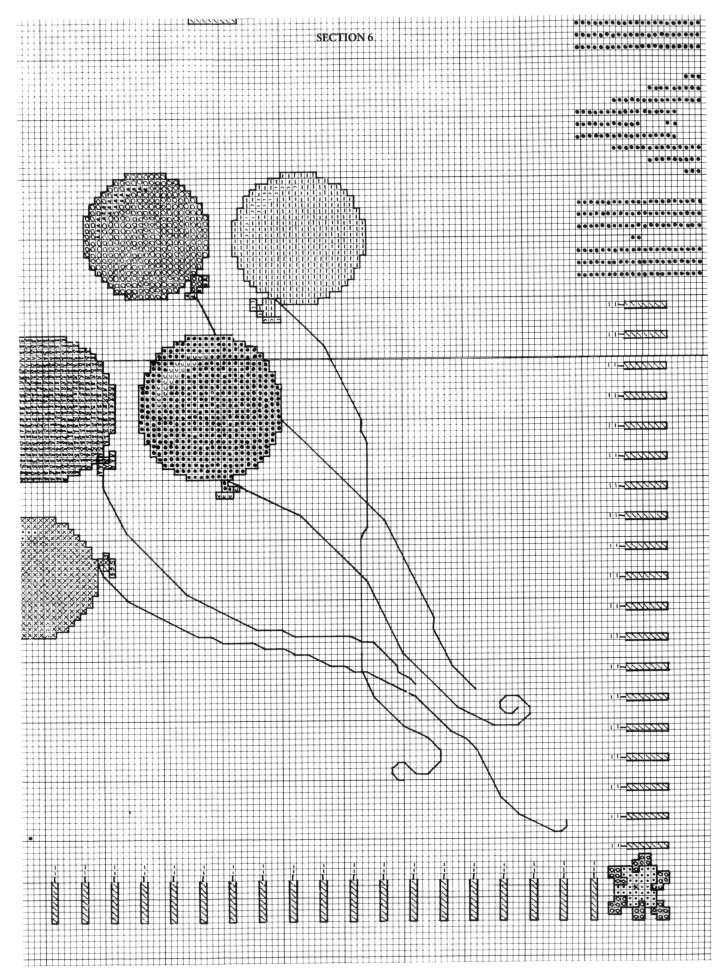

TOP

SIDE PANEL

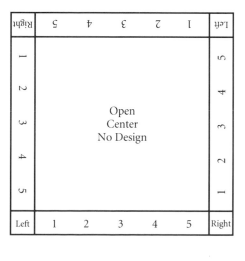

Right	5	4	3	2	1	Left
1						5
2						4
3			Open Center No Design			3
4						2
5						1
Left	1	2	3	4	5	Right

GRAPE ARBOR TABLECLOTH

DMC Coats Anchor®

w [823   7982   150   navy blue, dk.
    550   4107   102   violet, vy. dk.

6 [333   —   119   blue violet, dk.
    550   4107   102   violet, vy. dk.

∕ [333   —   119   blue violet, dk.
    552   4092   101   violet, dk.

− [554   4104   96   violet, lt.
    553   4097   98   violet, med.

■ [934   6270   862   avocado-black
    3371   5478   382   black-brown

● 3011   —   845   khaki, dk.

x 3012   —   844   khaki, med.

∖ 3013   —   842   khaki, lt.

z [610   —   889   drab brown, vy. lt.
    3011   —   845   khaki, dk.

Shaded portion indicates overlap from previous page.

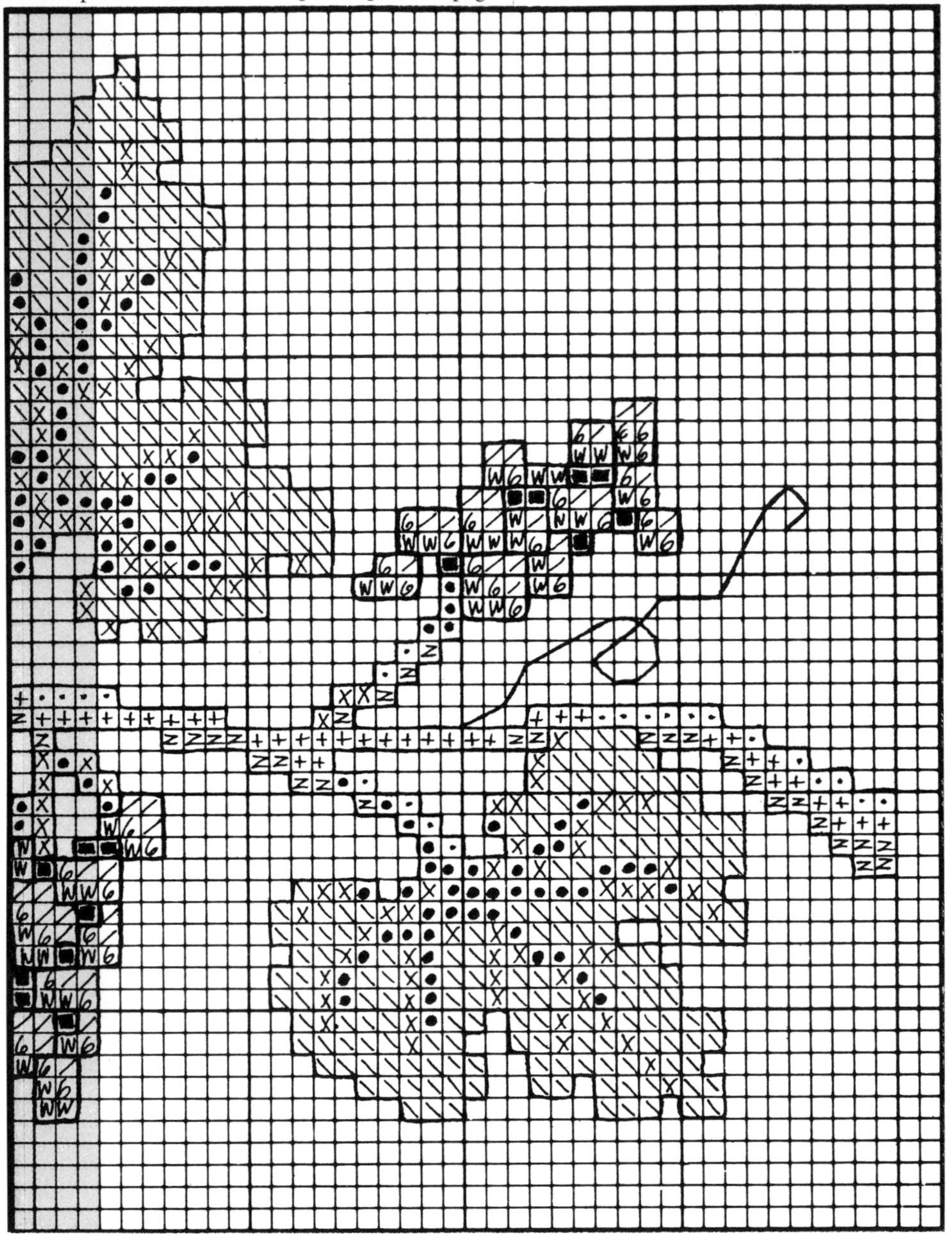

+ [611	—	898	drab brown, dk.
[3012	—	844	khaki, med.
• [612	—	832	drab brown, med.
[3013	—	842	khaki, lt.

Fabric used for model: 14-count Louisiana white from Wichelt Imports, Inc.
Stitch count:
Corner design—64H x 64W
Side Panel—52H x 100W
Approximate design size:
Corner design—4 ½" x 4 ½"
Side panel—3 ¾" x 7"

NOTE: Set floss color before beginning, referring to "General Instructions and Helpful Hints." Instructions: Cross stitch using three strands of floss. Backstitch using one strand of floss. When two colors are bracketed together, use two strands of the first color and one strand of the second. Center LEFT grape design in lower left-hand corner, within woven border. To begin SIDE PANEL, shown on pages 75-76, count in 7 squares (to the right) and up 21 squares (from the bottom) from inside edge of woven border. Repeat design five times. Stitch RIGHT corner grape design, shown on page 78. Turn piece and stitch side panel design as above. Continue turning piece until design is completed. To finish, machine stitch 2 ½" from outside edge of woven border around perimeter of tablecloth. Fringe by pulling thread from edges to machine stitching.
Backstitch (bs) instructions:

823	7982	150	grapes
3011	—	845	leaves
610	—	889	stems
3012	—	844	vines on side panels

Designed by Cathy Livingston

Color code has been duplicated from previous page for stitching convenience.

GRAPE ARBOR TABLECLOTH

	DMC	Coats	Anchor®	
w [	823	7982	150	navy blue, dk.
	550	4107	102	violet, vy. dk.
6 [	333	—	119	blue violet, dk.
	550	4107	102	violet, vy. dk.
⁄ [	333	—	119	blue violet, dk.
	552	4092	101	violet, dk.
– [	554	4104	96	violet, lt.
	553	4097	98	violet, med.
■ [	934	6270	862	avocado-black
	3371	5478	382	black-brown

●	3011	—	845	khaki, dk.
x	3012		844	khaki, med.
╲	3013		842	khaki, lt.
z [	610		889	drab brown, vy. lt.
	3011		845	khaki, dk.
+ [	611		898	drab brown, dk.
	3012		844	khaki, med.
• [	612		832	drab brown, med.
	3013		842	khaki, lt.

Fabric used for model: 14-count Louisiana white from Wichelt Imports, Inc.

Color code has been duplicated from previous page for stitching convenience.

GRAPE ARBOR TABLECLOTH

	DMC	Coats	Anchor®	
w	823	7982	150	navy blue, dk.
	550	4107	102	violet, vy. dk.
6	333	—	119	blue violet, dk.
	550	4107	102	violet, vy. dk.
/	333	—	119	blue violet, dk.
	552	4092	101	violet, dk.
–	554	4104	96	violet, lt.
	553	4097	98	violet, med.
■	934	6270	862	avocado-black
	3371	5478	382	black-brown

	DMC		Anchor	
●	3011	—	845	khaki, dk.
x	3012	—	844	khaki, med.
\	3013	—	842	khaki, lt.
z	610	—	889	drab brown, vy. lt.
	3011	—	845	khaki, dk.
+	611	—	898	drab brown, dk.
	3012	—	844	khaki, med.
·	612	—	832	drab brown, med.
	3013	—	842	khaki, lt.

Fabric used for model: 14-count Louisiana white from Wichelt Imports, Inc.

SECTION 1

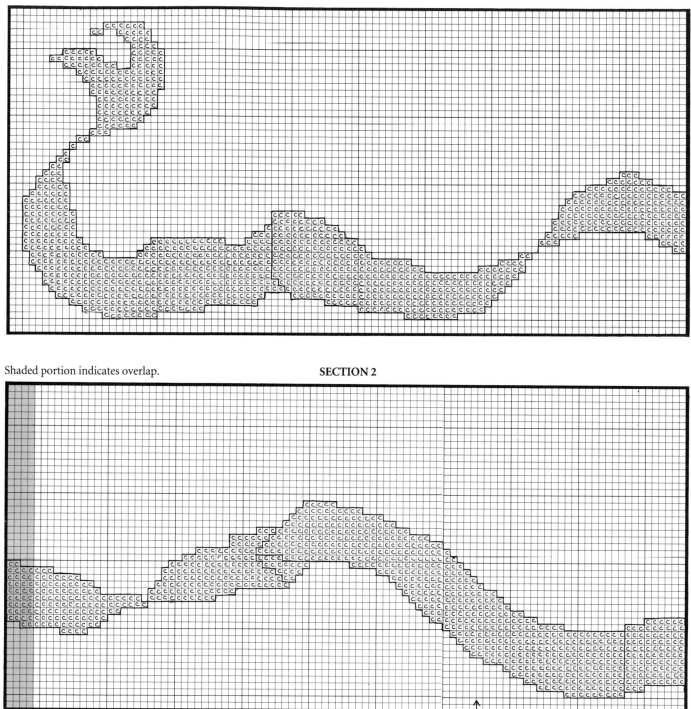

Shaded portion indicates overlap.

SECTION 2

Shaded portion indicates overlap from previous page.

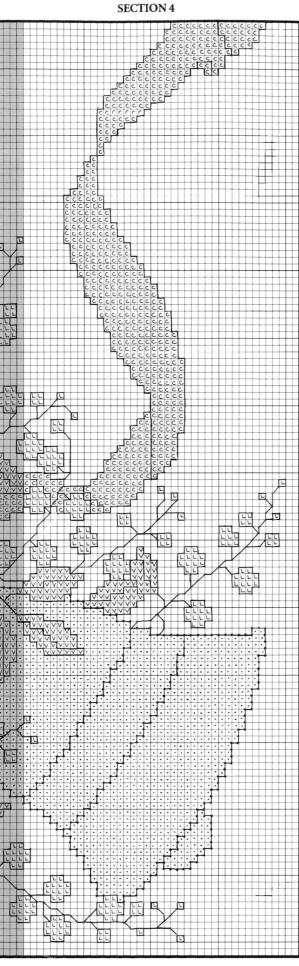

Shaded portion indicates overlap from previous page.

WEDDING BELLS TABLECLOTH

	DMC	Balger®	
•	white		white
L	3753		antique blue, vy. lt.
c	225		pink, vy. lt.
V	504		blue green, lt.
bs [		002	gold
	676		old gold, lt.
bs [		001	silver
	415		pearl gray

Fabric used for model: 28-count white linen from Charles Craft, Inc.
Stitch count: 330H x 330W
Approximate design size: 23 ⅝" x 23 ⅝"

Instructions: Cross stitch over two threads using three strands of floss. Backstitch using one strand each of floss and Balger® blending filament.
Backstitch (bs) instructions:

····[Balger 002
[676

— [Balger 001
[415

Finishing Instructions:
1. Purchase 60" x 60" piece of fabric, 7 yds. complementary lace of your choice, and matching thread.
2. Center design 2" from raw edge of fabric and stitch, following instructions given.
3. To finish, make a shirttail hem around perimeter of tablecloth, and attach lace over hem, mitering at corners.

Designed by Linda Jary

SECTION 5

SECTION 6

Shaded portion indicates overlap from previous page.

Shaded portion indicates overlap.

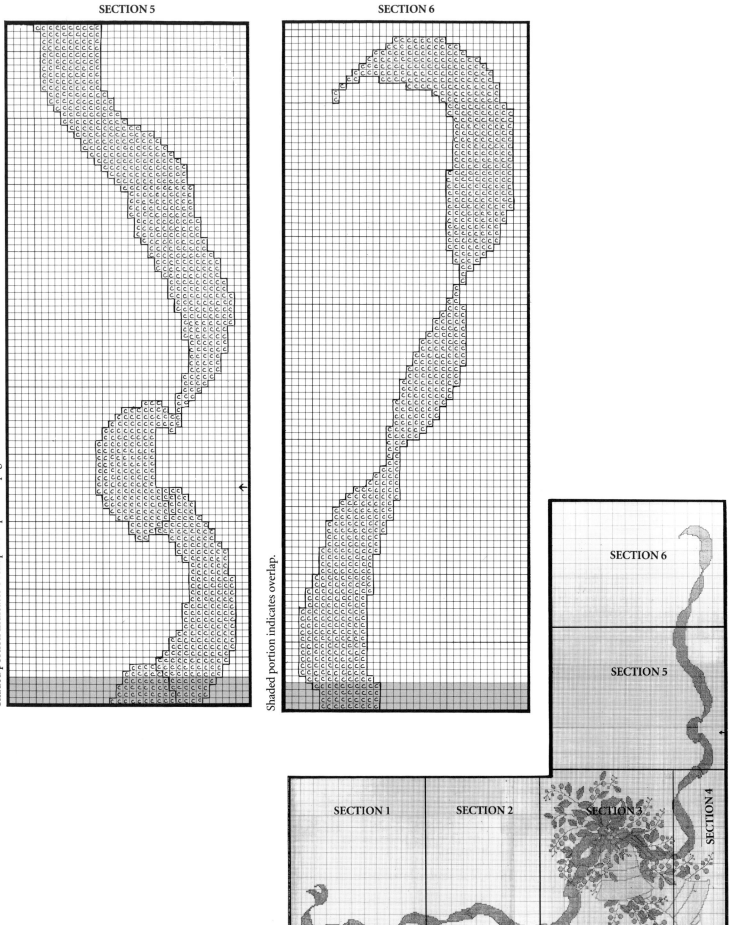

SECTION 6

SECTION 5

SECTION 4

SECTION 1

SECTION 2

SECTION 3

82

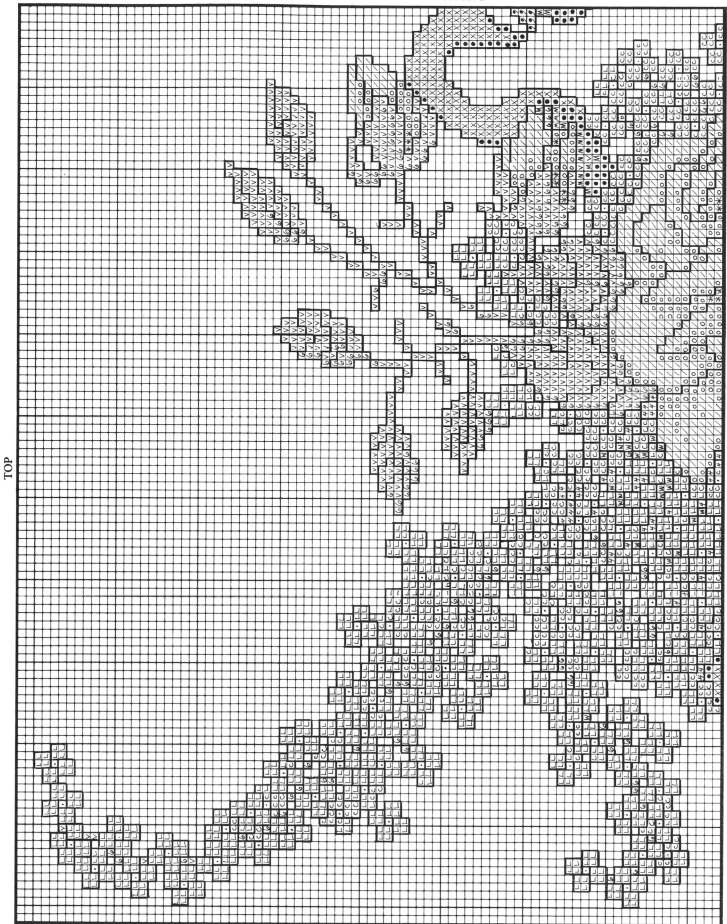

TOP

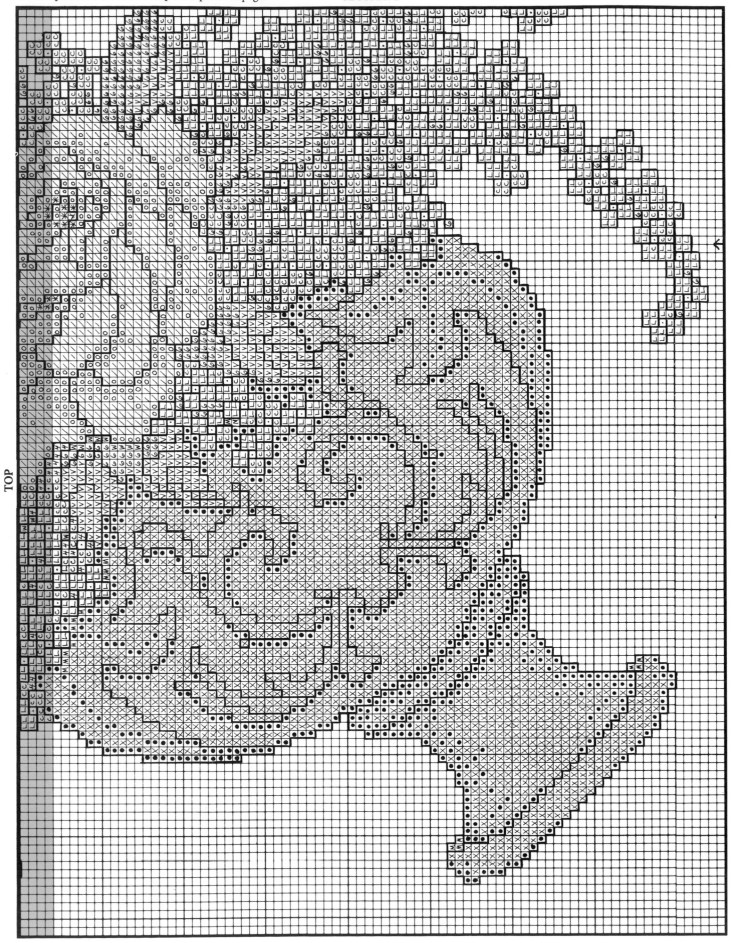

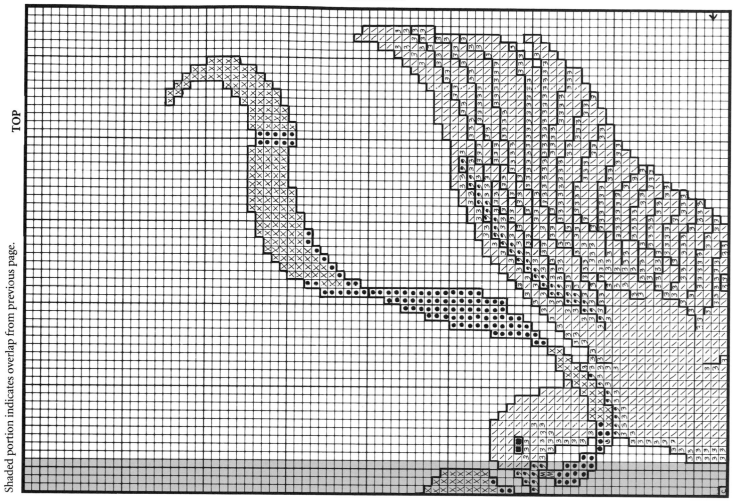

TOP

Shaded portion indicates overlap from previous page.

CELEBRATIONS

	DMC	Coats	Anchor®	
x	677	—	886	old gold, vy. lt.,
●	676	2305	887	old gold, lt.
M	729		874	old gold, mcd.
∕	819	3280	271	baby pink, lt.
o	818	3281	23	baby pink
✳	776	3281	25	pink, med.
V	369	6015	260	pistachio, vy. lt.
6	367	6018	210	pistachio, dk.
L	747	7053	928	sky blue, vy. lt.
c	3761	—	9159	sky blue, lt.
•	3078	2292	292	golden yellow, vy. lt.
५	519	—	168	sky blue
w	320	607	215	pistachio, med.
೨	642	—	832	beige-gray, dk.
3	644	—	831	beige-gray, med.
∖	822	—	830	beige-gray, lt.
■	611	—	898	drab brown, dk.

Fabric used for model: 26-count white Super Linen from Charles Craft, Inc.
Stitch count: 164H x 164W
Approximate design size:
14-count—11 ¾" x 11 ¾"
18-count—9 ⅛" x 9 ⅛"
26-count—12 ⅝" x 12 ⅝"
30-count—10 ⅞" x 10 ⅞"

Instructions: Cross stitch over two threads using three strands of floss. Backstitch using two strands 611/—/898.
Finishing instructions:
1. Purchase 60" x 60" piece of fabric, 7 yds. complementary lace, and matching thread.
2. Center design 2 ½" from raw edge of fabric and stitch, following instructions given.
3. To finish, make a shirttail hem around perimeter of tablecloth, and attach lace over hem, mitering at corners.

Designed by Linda Jary

TOP

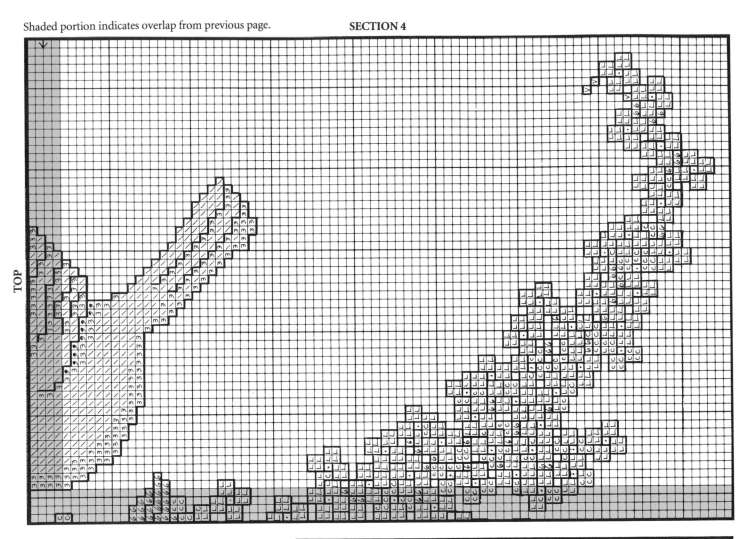

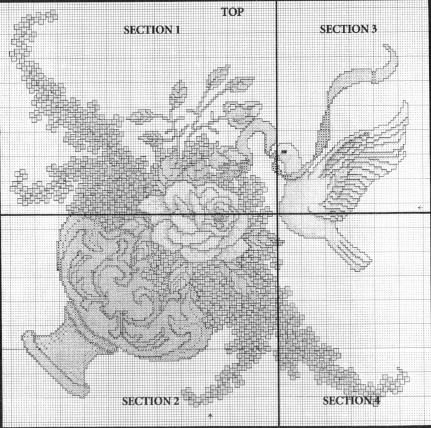

86

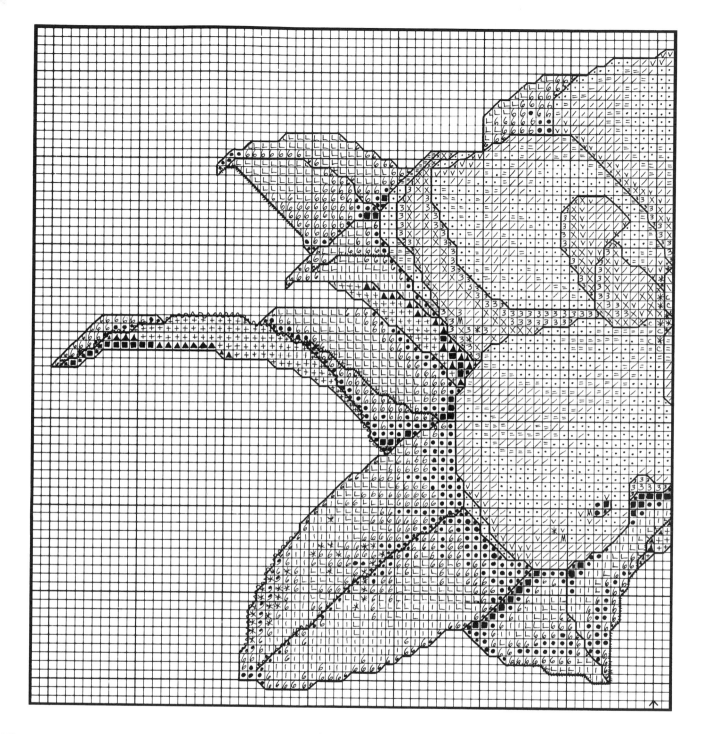

MAGNOLIA BLOSSOM TABLE RUNNER

DMC Coats Anchor®

•	white	1001	01	white

=[white 1001 01 white
   712 5387 926 cream

/[white 1001 01 white
   948 2331 778 peach flesh, vy. lt.

V[3033 5388 388 mocha, vy. lt.
   948 2331 778 peach flesh, vy. lt.

x[3033 5388 388 mocha, vy. lt.
   3024 8390 900 brown-gray, vy. lt.

3 3024 8390 900 brown-gray, vy. lt.

✳ 420 5374 374 hazelnut, dk.

M[420 5374 374 hazelnut, dk.
   3045 2412 886 yellow-beige, dk.

c[3045 2412 886 yellow-beige, dk.
   3046 2410 888 yellow-beige, med.

╲[3046 2410 888 yellow-beige, med.
   3047 2300 956 yellow-beige, lt.

≠[420 5374 374 hazelnut, dk.
   834 — 945 olive, vy. lt.

> 834 — 945 olive, vy. lt.

•[890 6021 212 pistachio, ul. dk.
   934 6270 862 avocado-black

6 890 6021 212 pistachio, ul. dk.

L 319 6246 246 pistachio, vy. dk.

ı[367 6018 210 pistachio, dk.
   320 6017 215 pistachio, med.

+[300 — 352 mahogany, vy. dk.
   838 5381 380 beige-brown, vy. dk.

◗ 433 5471 944 brown, med.

▲ 838 5381 380 beige-brown, vy. dk.

■ 3371 5478 382 black-brown

bs 647 8900 8581 beaver gray, med.

Fabric used for model: 26-count white Sal-Em
cloth pre-finished table runner from Carolina
Cross Stitch, Inc.

Stitch count: 74H x 140W

Shaded portion indicates overlap from previous page.

Approximate design size:	433	5471	944	center of flower

Approximate design size:
  26-count—5 ¾" x 10 ¾"
  28-count—5 ¼" x 10"
  30-count—5" x 9 ⅜"
  32-count—4 ⅝" x 8 ¾"

Instructions: Cross stitch over two threads using two strands of floss. Backstitch using one strand of floss. When two colors are bracketed together, use one strand of each. NOTE: Center design 1" up from fabric edge, using center of design as a guide for placement.
Backstitch (bs) instructions: Backstitch in order listed.

433	5471	944	center of flower
647	8900	8581	petals
+++ 320	6017	215	leaves (where symbol appears)
ʌʌʌ 433	5471	944	leaves (where symbol appears)
890	6021	212	remainder of leaves
3371	5478	382	stem

Designed by Cathy Livingston

Shaded portion indicates overlap from previous page.

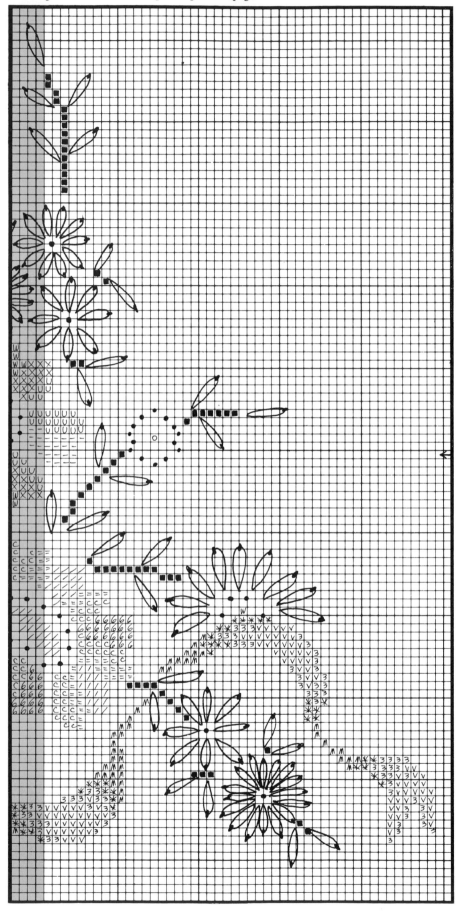

GRANDMA HILL'S BOUQUET

Pastel Color Code

	DMC	Coats	Anchor®	
■	988	6258	244	forest, dk.
M	312	7979	979	navy, lt.
✳	322	7978	978	navy, vy. lt.
3	334	7977	977	baby blue, med.
V	3325	7976	144	baby blue
6	335	3283	38	rose
c	899	3282	38	rose, med.
=	776	3281	25	pink, med.
╱	818	3281	23	baby pink
z	209	4302	110	lavender, dk.
o	210	4303	108	lavender, med.
╲	211	4303	342	lavender, lt.
w	783	—	307	gold
∪	726	2294	295	topaz, lt.
−	746	—	275	off white
LD	989	6266	242	forest
x	725	2298	305	topaz

Fabric used for model: 26-count white Sal-Em cloth pre-finished table runner from Carolina Cross Stitch, Inc.

Lazy Daisy (LD) instructions: When three colors are bracketed together, use one strand of each.

989	6266	242	all leaves on stems

Areas 1:

899	3282	38	pink flowers
776	3281	25	
818	3281	23	

Areas 2:

209	4302	110	purple flowers
210	4303	108	
211	4303	342	

Areas 3:

322	7978	978	blue flowers
344	7977	977	
3325	7976	144	

Areas 4:

725	2298	305	yellow flowers
726	2294	295	
746	—	275	

French knots:

899	3282	38	areas 1
209	4302	110	areas 2
322	7978	978	areas 3
725	2298	305	areas 4
211	4303	342	center of large purple flower (*A*)
726	2294	295	center of large yellow flower (*B*)
776	3281	25	center of large pink flower (*C*)

Antique Color Code

	DMC	Coats	Anchor®	
■	319	6246	246	pistachio, vy. dk.
M	930	7052	922	antique blue, dk.
*	931	7051	921	antique blue, med.
3	932	7050	343	antique blue, lt.
V	3752	—	976	antique blue
6	347	3013	13	salmon, dk.
c	3328	3071	10	salmon, med.
=	3712	—	—	salmon, med. dk.
/	760	3069	894	salmon
z	3041	4222	871	antique violet, med.
o	3042	4221	869	antique violet, lt.
\	3743	—	869	antique violet, vy. lt.
w	729	—	874	old gold, lt.
x	676	2305	877	old gold, lt.
∪	677	—	886	old gold, vy. lt.
‐	745	2296	300	yellow, lt. pale
LD	367	6018	210	pistachio, dk.

Fabric used for model: 26-count ecru Sal-Em cloth pre-finished table runner from Carolina Cross Stitch, Inc.

Lazy Daisy (LD) instructions: When three colors are bracketed together, use one strand of each.

| | 367 | 6018 | 210 | all leaves on stems |

Areas 1:

	3328	3071	10	pink flowers
	3712	—	—	
	760	3069	894	

Areas 2:

	3041	4222	871	purple flowers
	3042	4221	869	
	3743	—	869	

Areas 3:

	931	7051	921	blue flowers
	932	7050	343	
	3752	—	976	

Areas 4:

	676	2305	877	yellow flowers
	677	—	886	
	745	2296	300	

French knots:

3328	3071	10	areas 1
3041	4222	871	areas 2
931	7051	343	areas 3
676	2305	877	areas 4
3743	—	869	center of large purple flower (A)
677	—	886	center of large yellow flower (B)
3712	—	—	center of large pink flower (C)

Stitch count: 105H x 133W
Approximate design size:
26-count—8" x 10 ¼"
27-count—7 ¾" x 9 ⅞"
28-count—7 ½" x 9 ½"
32-count—6 ⅝" x 8 ⅜"

Instructions: Cross stitch over two threads using two strands of floss. Make Lazy Daisy (LD) stitches using three strands of floss. Make French knots using two strands of floss, wrapping floss around needle twice. NOTE: There is no backstitching in this design.
Refer to illustration for placement of special stitches.
Designed by Cathy Livingston

LAZY DAISY STITCH

To work Lazy Daisy stitch, bring needle up at 1, and go down at 2 (in the same hole), leaving a loop in the floss. Then bring needle up at 3, pulling up slack in floss loop, and go down at 4 to secure loop.

REINDEER AND RIBBON TABLE RUNNER

DMC Coats Anchor®
● white 1001 01 white

Fabric used for model: 25-count Christmas red
Lugana® from Zweigart®
Stitch count: 95H x 92W

Approximate design size:
  14-count—6 ¾" x 6 ⅝"
  18-count—5 ¼" x 5 ⅛"
  22-count—4 ⅜" x 4 ¼"
  25-count—7 ⅝" x 7 ⅜"

NOTE: Pre-wash fabric to set color, and pre-shrink lace before beginning. Cut fabric 16 ½" x

42". Stitch design at both ends, leaving 3 ½" below design to edge of fabric.

Instructions: Cross stitch over two threads using three strands of floss. Backstitch using two strands white. Design may be stitched on white fabric using floss color of your choice.

Designed by Cathy Livingston

BOUNTIFUL HARVEST TABLE RUNNER

	DMC	Coats	Anchor®	
3	920	3337	339	copper, med.
o	720	—	326	spice, dk.
\	970	2327	316	pumpkin, lt.
◤	498	3410	43	red, dk.
	934	6270	862	avocado-black
N	498	3410	43	red, dk.
–	304	3401	19	red, med.
	349	2335	13	coral, dk.
z	733	—	280	olive, med.
	783	—	307	gold
∟	734	—	279	olive, lt.
	725	2298	305	topaz
II	726	2294	295	topaz, lt.
●	3371	5478	382	black-brown
➒	936	6269	269	avocado, vy. dk.
*	3011	—	845	khaki, dk.
>	3012	—	844	khaki, med.
I	3013	—	842	khaki, lt.
6	550	4107	102	violet, vy. dk.
	327	4101	100	violet, dk.
x	552	4092	101	violet, dk.
	3740	—	—	antique violet
/	554	4104	96	violet, lt.
	3041	4222	871	antique violet, med.
■	823	7982	150	navy, dk.
	902	3083	897	garnet, vy. dk.
w	902	3083	897	garnet, vy. dk.
//	815	3000	22	garnet, med.
▼	730	—	924	olive, vy. dk.
	831	—	277	olive, med.
ʞ	732	—	281	olive
	832	—	907	olive
⟍	834	—	945	olive, vy. lt.
∧	730	—	924	olive, vy. dk.
⊙	732	—	281	olive
◢	3371	5478	382	black-brown
	801	5475	353	coffee, dk.
M	801	5475	353	coffee, dk.
ⴂ	434	5000	370	brown, lt.
V	435	5371	363	brown, vy. lt.
=	437	5942	361	tan, lt.
•	738	5375	372	tan, vy. lt.

Fabric used for model: 26-count 13" x 38" cream linen table runner with fringe from Carolina Cross Stitch, Inc.

Stitch count: 92H x 110W

Approximate design size:
- 14-count—6 ⅝" x 7 ⅞"
- 18-count—5 ⅛" x 6 ⅛"
- 26-count—7 ⅛" x 8 ½"
- 27-count—6 ¾" x 8 ⅛"
- 32-count—5 ¾" x 6 ⅞"

Instructions: Cross stitch over two threads using two strands of floss. Backstitch using one strand of floss unless indicated otherwise.

NOTE: Center design 1" from fabric edge using center of design as a guide for placement.

Backstitch (bs) instructions:

3011	—	845	grape tendrils (two strands)
801	5475	353	stems on pear, apples, and cherries (two strands)
3371	5478	382	remainder of backstitching

Designed by Cathy Livingston

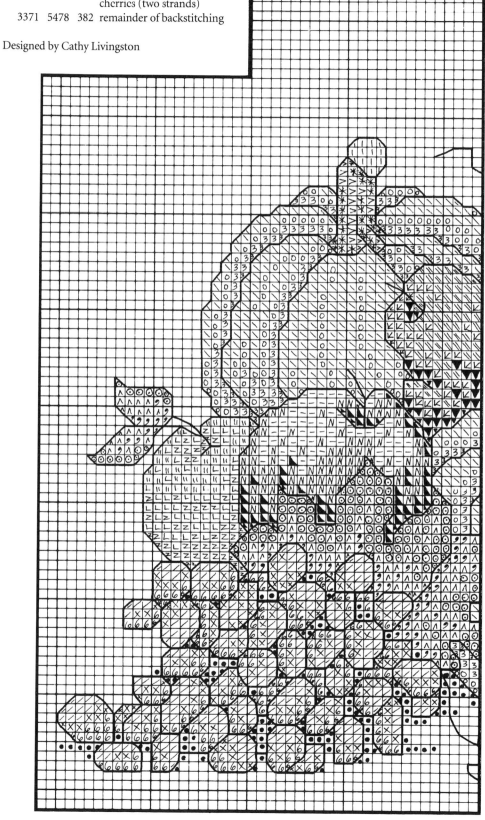

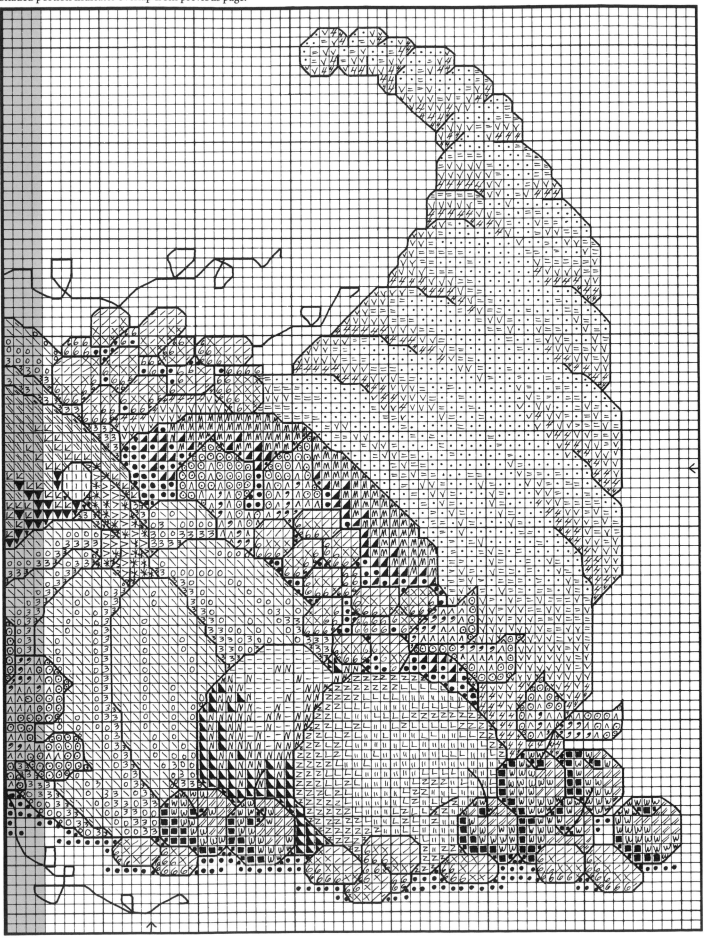

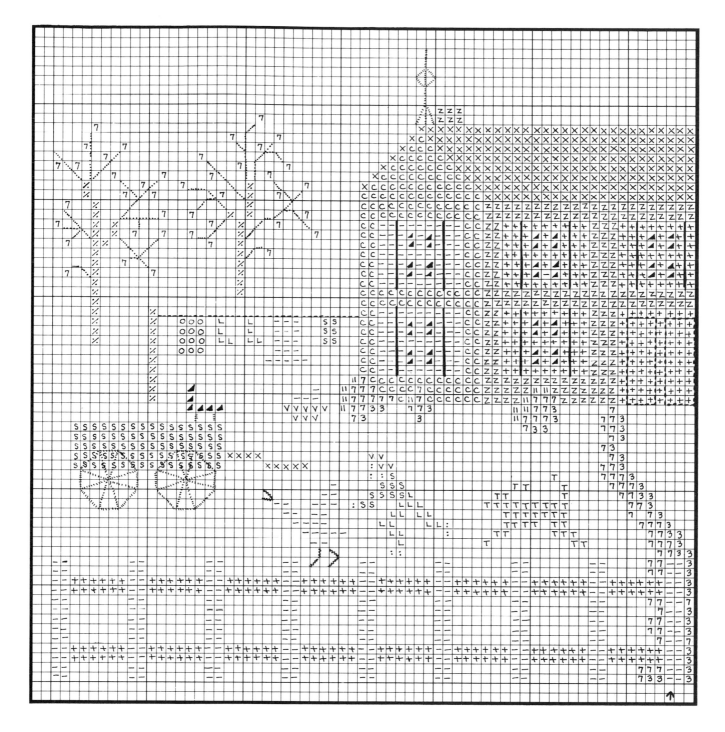

PRIMITIVE TABLE RUNNER

DMC Coats Anchor®

	DMC	Coats	Anchor	
−	white	1001	01	white
●	310	8403	403	black
L	931	7051	921	antique blue, med.
x	413	8514	236	pewter gray, dk.
‖	3348	6266	264	yellow-green, lt.
7	3347	6266	267	yellow-green, med.
3	3346	6258	268	hunter
o	3752	—	976	antique blue
c	921	—	349	copper
z	920	3337	339	copper, med.
s	347	3013	13	salmon, dk.
꞉	951	3335	933	flesh, vy. lt.

	DMC	Coats	Anchor	
+	3072	6005	234	beaver gray, vy. lt.
◢	318	8511	399	steel gray, lt.
T	434	5000	370	brown, lt.
⁒	801	5475	353	coffee, dk.
V	676	2305	887	old gold, lt.
✱	727	2289	293	topaz, vy. lt.
bs	355	2339	5975	terra cotta, dk.
bs	720	—	326	spice, dk.

Fabric used for model: 14-count parchment Yorkshire Aida from Zweigart®
Stitch count: 66H x 130W
Approximate design size:
    14-count—4 ¾" x 9 ¼"

Instructions: Cross stitch using three strands of floss. Backstitch using two strands of floss. NOTE: Cut fabric 33" x 11 ¾ ". Stitch design at both ends, leaving 1" below design to edge of fabric. Machine stitch ½" in from edge on all sides. Fringe by pulling threads from edges to machine stitching.
Backstitch (bs) instructions:

	DMC	Coats	Anchor
—	355	2339	5975
∿∿	720	—	326
‖‖‖‖	310	8403	403
••••	801	5475	353
----	318	8511	399

Designed by Linda Jary

Shaded portion indicates overlap from previous page.

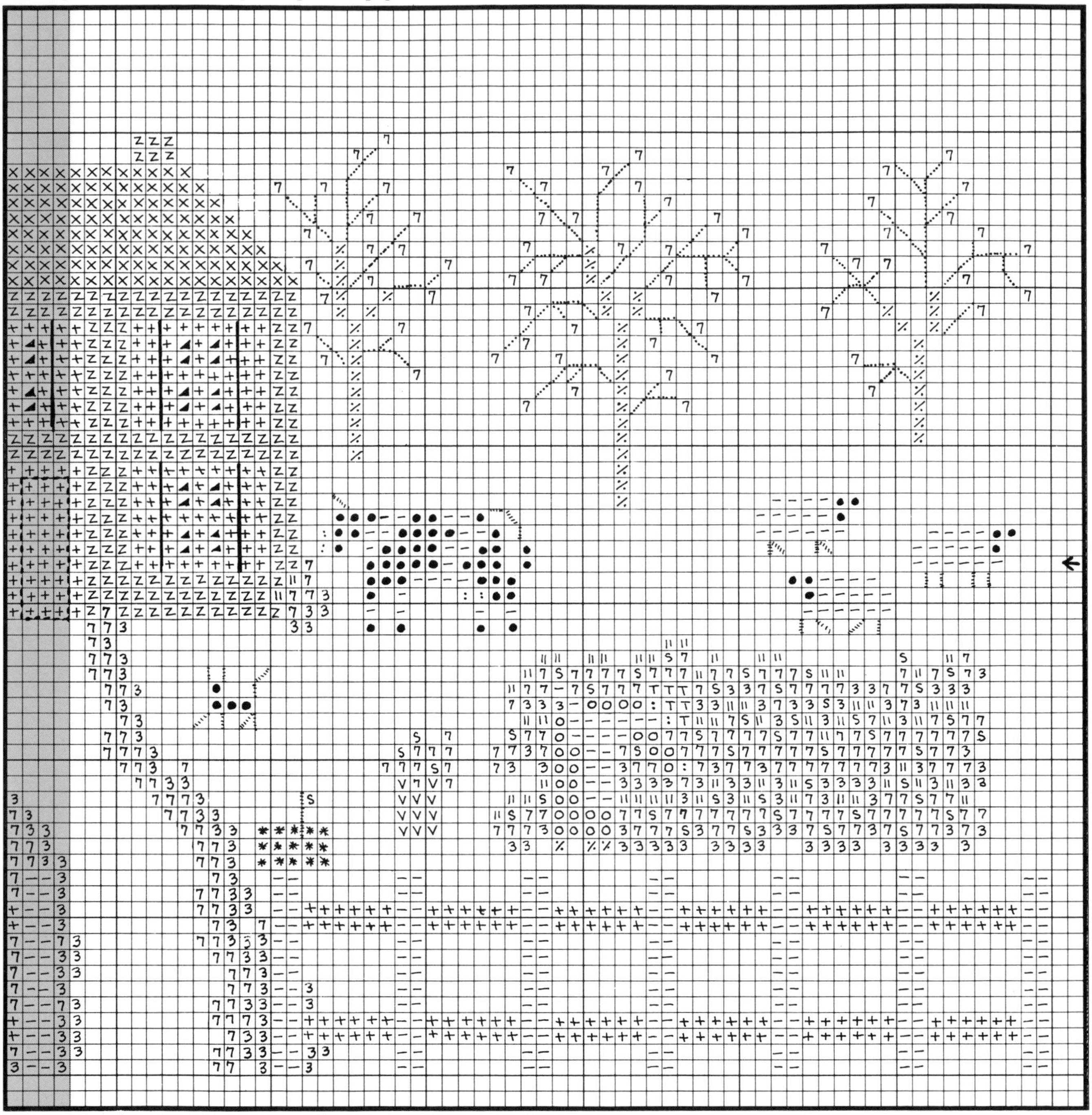

PARASOL BOUQUET DRESSER SCARF

	DMC	Coats	Anchor®	
o	744	2293	301	yellow, pl.
=	3689	3086	49	mauve, lt.
V	341	7005	117	blue violet, lt.
•	white	1001	01	white

╱	762	8510	397	pearl gray, vy. lt.
∪	415	8510	398	pearl gray
z	318	8511	399	steel gray, lt.
x	772	6250	253	pine green, lt.
bs	414	8513	235	steel gray, dk.
bs	3688	3087	66	mauve, med.
bs	340	7110	118	blue violet, med.
bs	725	2298	305	topaz

Fabric used for model: 28-count periwinkle blue linen from Zweigart®

Stitch count: 102H x 160W

Approximate design size:

27-count—7 ½" x 11 ⅞"
28-count—7 ¼" x 11 ⅜"
30-count—6 ⅞" x 10 ⅝"
32-count—6 ⅜" x 10"

Instructions: Cross stitch over two threads using two strands of floss. Backstitch using one strand of floss.

NOTE: Stitch design at both ends, leaving 3 ½" below design to edge of fabric. When stitching is complete, finish with a ¼" hem. Hemstitching shown was done using a Bernina®, model 1230.

When hemstitching is desired, pull threads before hemming.

Backstitch (bs) instructions:

—	414	8513	235
∧∧∧	3688	3087	66
••••	340	7110	118
‖‖‖	725	2298	305

Designed by Linda Jary

FOUR FLOWERS ON NAVY
DAYLILY AND BEETLES PLACE MAT

	DMC	Coats	Anchor®	
-	746	—	275	off white
T	472	6253	264	avocado, ul. lt.
c	471	6010	266	avocado, vy. lt.
V	470	6010	267	avocado, lt.
:	677	—	886	old gold, vy. lt.
N	676	2305	887	old gold, lt.
3	729	—	874	old gold, med.
J	818	3281	23	baby pink
ll	819	3280	271	baby pink, lt.
o	963	3280	73	dusty rose, vy. lt.
x	502	6876	877	blue green
z	501	6878	878	blue green, dk.
7	434	5000	370	brown, lt.
bs	603	3001	62	cranberry
bs	801	5475	353	coffee, dk.
bs	469	6261	268	avocado

Fabric used for model: 28-count navy Jobelan from Wichelt Imports, Inc.
Stitch count: 147H x 224W
Approximate design size:
28-count—10 ½" x 16"

NOTE: Corners of border are shown for centering flowers in main design.
Instructions: Cross stitch over two threads using three strands of floss. Backstitch using two strands of floss. Cut fabric 12 ½" x 18". Machine stitch ½" from cut edge on all sides. Fringe by pulling threads from edges to machine stitching.
Backstitch (bs) instructions:

—	603	3001	62
∞	801	5475	353
cccc	677	—	886
lllll	471	6010	266
••••	470	6010	267
ʌʌ	469	6261	268
----	502	6876	877

IRIS AND MOTH PLACE MAT

	DMC	Coats	Anchor®	
L {	472	6253	264	avocado, ul. lt. (two strands)
	445	2288	288	lemon, lt. (one strand)
T	472	6253	264	avocado, ul. lt.
c	471	6010	266	avocado, vy. lt.
:	3747	—	—	blue violet, ul. lt.
o	341	7005	117	blue violet, lt.
3	340	7110	118	blue violet, med.
z	333	—	119	blue violet, dk.
=	744	2293	301	yellow, pl.
h	742	2303	303	tangerine, lt.
ll	503	6879	876	blue green, med.
x	502	6876	877	blue green
∪	501	6878	878	blue green, dk.
-	739	5369	942	tan, ul. lt.
7	738	5375	372	tan, vy. lt.
V	470	6010	267	avocado, lt.
+	976	2308	309	gold brown, med.
bs	3746	—	—	blue-violet

bs 469 6261 268 avocado
bs 975 5349 355 golden-brown, dk.

Fabric used for model: 28-count navy Jobelan from Wichelt Imports, Inc.
Stitch count: 147H x 224W
Approximate design size:
28-count—10 ½" x 16"

NOTE: Corners of border are shown for centering flowers in main design.
Instructions: Cross stitch over two threads using three strands of floss. Backstitch using two strands of floss. When two colors are bracketed together, blend as indicated. Cut fabric 12 ½" x 18". Machine stitch ½" from cut edge on all sides. Fringe by pulling threads from edges to machine stitching.
Backstitch (bs) instructions:

—	3746	—	—
lllll	471	6010	266
••••	470	6010	267
ʌʌ	469	6261	268
••••	742	6253	264
----	502	6876	876
∞	738	5375	372
cccc	975	5349	355

JONQUILS AND SNAILS PLACE MAT

	DMC	Coats	Anchor®	
:	745	2296	300	yellow, lt. pl.
h	744	2293	301	yellow, pl.
=	743	2302	302	yellow, med.
N	742	2303	303	tangerine, lt.
x	740	2099	316	tangerine
z	834	—	945	olive, vy. lt.
T	472	6253	264	avocado, ul. lt.
c	471	6010	266	avocado, vy. lt.
y	470	6010	267	avocado, lt.
V	503	6879	876	blue green, med.
o	502	6876	877	blue green
∪	501	5878	878	blue green, dk.
•	937	6268	268	avocado, med.
7	738	5375	372	tan, vy. lt.
-	739	5369	942	tan, ul. lt.
■	3790	—	—	beige-gray
L	642	—	832	beige-gray, dk.
bs	469	6261	268	avocado
bs	437	5942	361	tan, lt.

Fabric used for model: 28-count navy blue Jobelan from Wichelt Imports, Inc.
Stitch count: 147H x 2224W
Approximate design size:
28-count: 10 ½" x 16"

NOTE: Corners of border are shown for centering flowers in main design.
Instructions: Cross stitch over two threads using three strands of floss. Backstitch using two strands of floss. Cut fabric 12 ½" x 18". Machine stitch ½" from cut edge on all sides. Fringe by pulling threads from edges to machine stitching.
Backstitch (bs) instructions:

—	740	2099	316	inside and around edge of *trumpet* in middle of flower
—	743	2302	302	yellow petals
lllll	470	6010	267
••••	469	6261	268
••••	937	6268	268
ʌʌ	437	5942	361
----	501	6878	878
--·--·	3790	—	—

TULIP AND DAMSELFLIES PLACE MAT

	DMC	Coats	Anchor®	
:	605	—	60	cranberry, vy. lt.
h	604	3001	86	cranberry, lt.
ll	603	3001	62	cranberry
x	602	3063	63	cranberry, med.
L	828	7053	158	blue, ul. lt.
T	472	6253	264	avocado, ul. lt.
c	471	6010	266	avocado, vy. lt.
y	470	6010	267	avocado, lt.
=	504	6875	857	blue green, lt.
V	503	6879	876	blue green, med.
o	502	6876	877	blue green
∪	501	6878	878	blue green, dk.
3	500	6880	879	blue green, vy. dk.
K	414	8513	235	steel, gray, dk.
z	601	3128	57	cranberry, dk.
bs	762	8510	397	pearl gray, vy. lt.

Fabric used for model: 28-count navy Jobelan from Wichelt Imports, Inc.
Stitch count: 147H x 224W
Approximate design size:
28-count—10 ½" x 16"

NOTE: Corners of border are shown for centering flowers in main design.
Instructions: Cross stitch over two threads using three strands of floss. Backstitch using two strands of floss. Cut fabric 18" x 12 ½". Enclose each flower in border as shown on chart for *Tulip and Damselflies* place mat. For each design, continue stitching border across top and bottom of place mat, stopping 1 ½" from right edge of fabric. Then stitch border closed on right-hand side, using the left-hand side of *Tulip and Damselflies* place mat chart as a guide for corners. Machine stitch ½" in from edge on all sides. Fringe by pulling threads from edges to machine stitching.
Backstitch (bs) instructions:

—	762	8510	397
••••	602	3063	63
lllll	470	6010	267
ʌʌ	503	6879	876
••••	502	6876	877
----	501	6878	878

Designed by Linda Jary

TULIP AND DAMSELFLIES PLACE MAT

TOP

JONQUILS AND SNAILS PLACE MAT

Shaded portion indicates overlap from previous page.

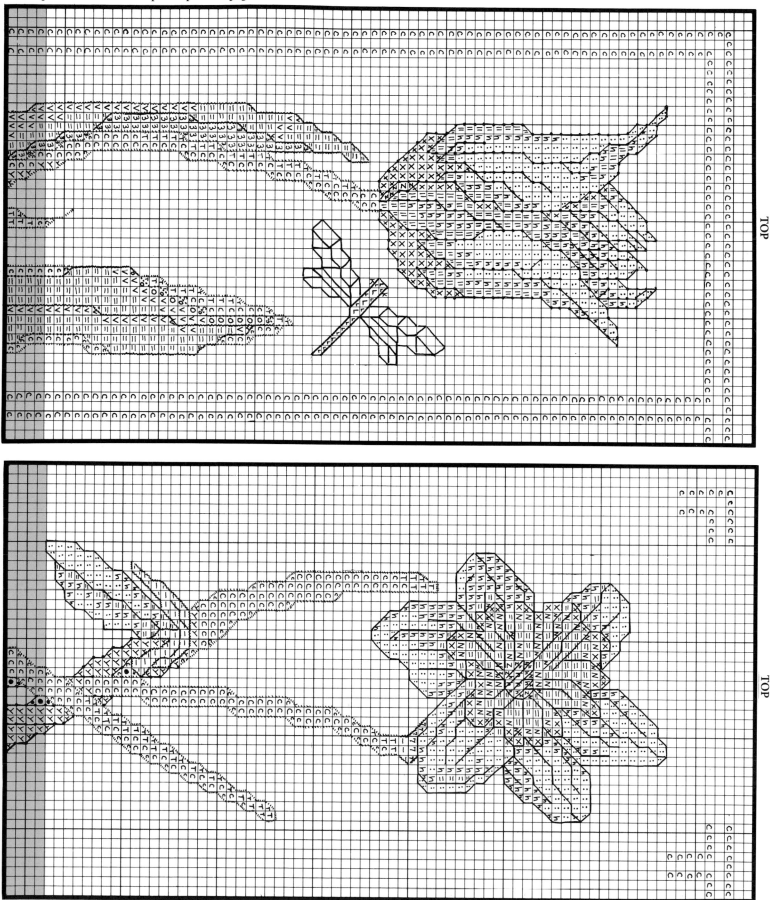

IRIS AND MOTH PLACE MAT

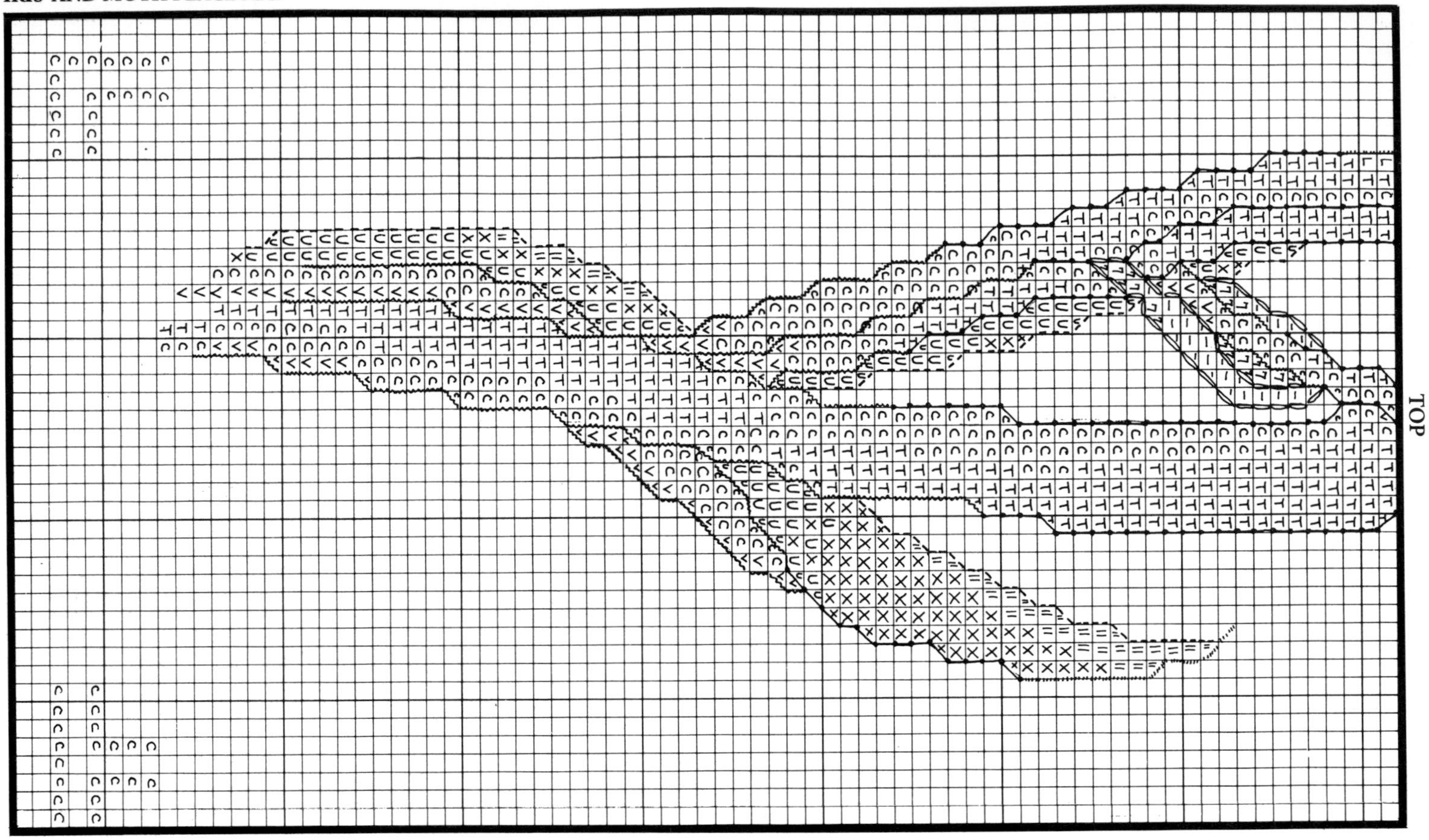

TOP

DAYLILY AND BEETLES PLACE MAT

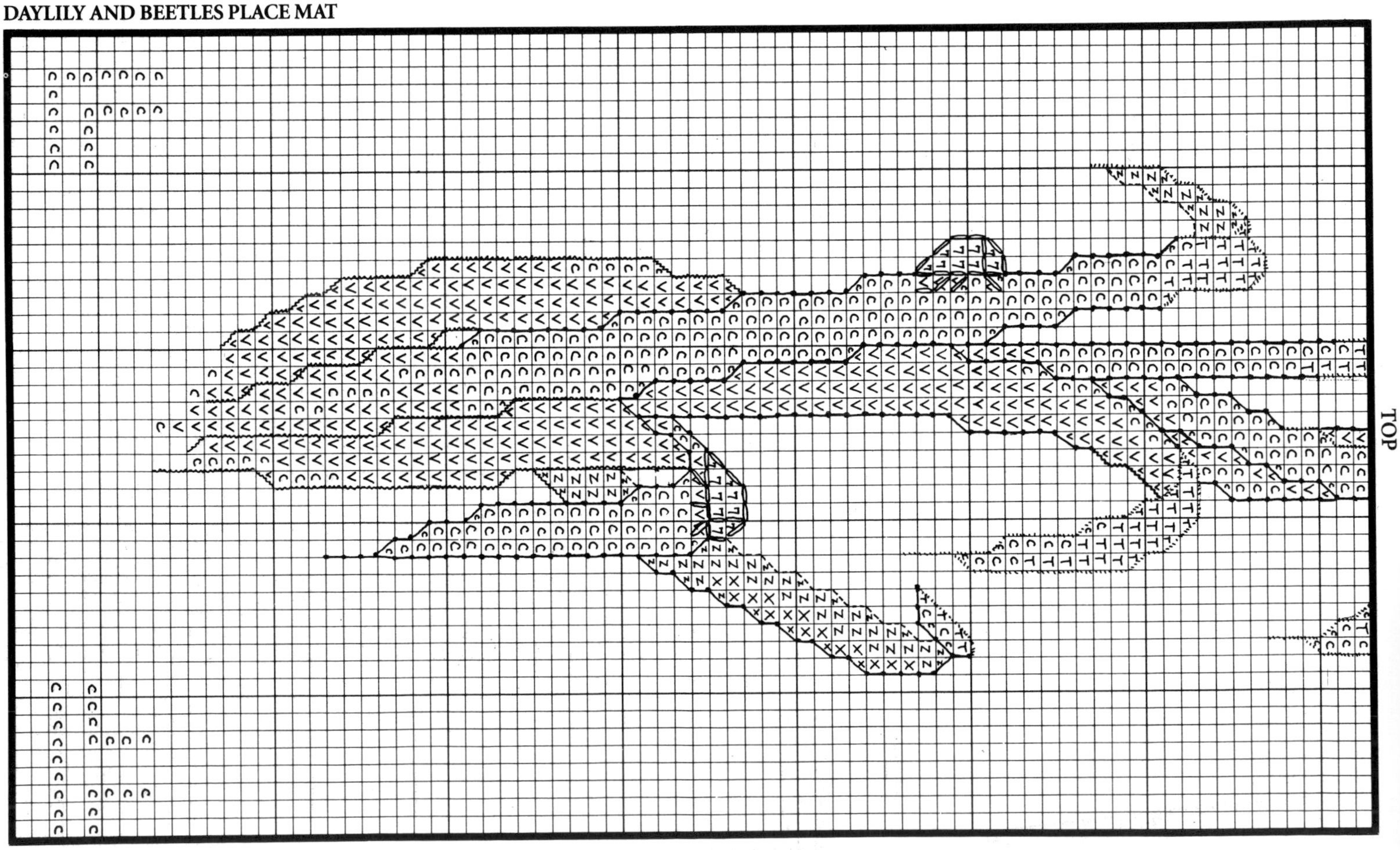

TOP

102

Shaded portion indicates overlap from previous page.

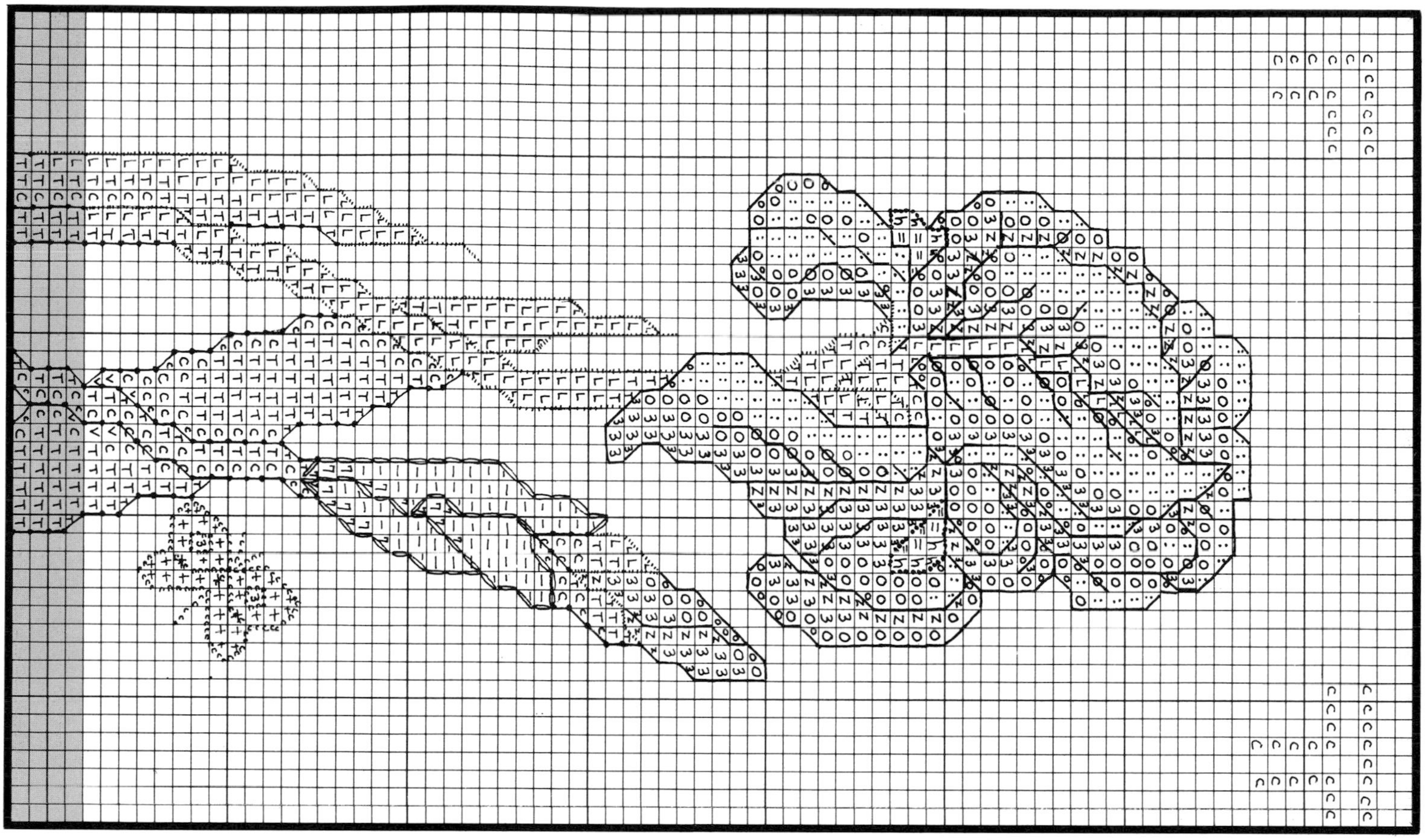

TOP

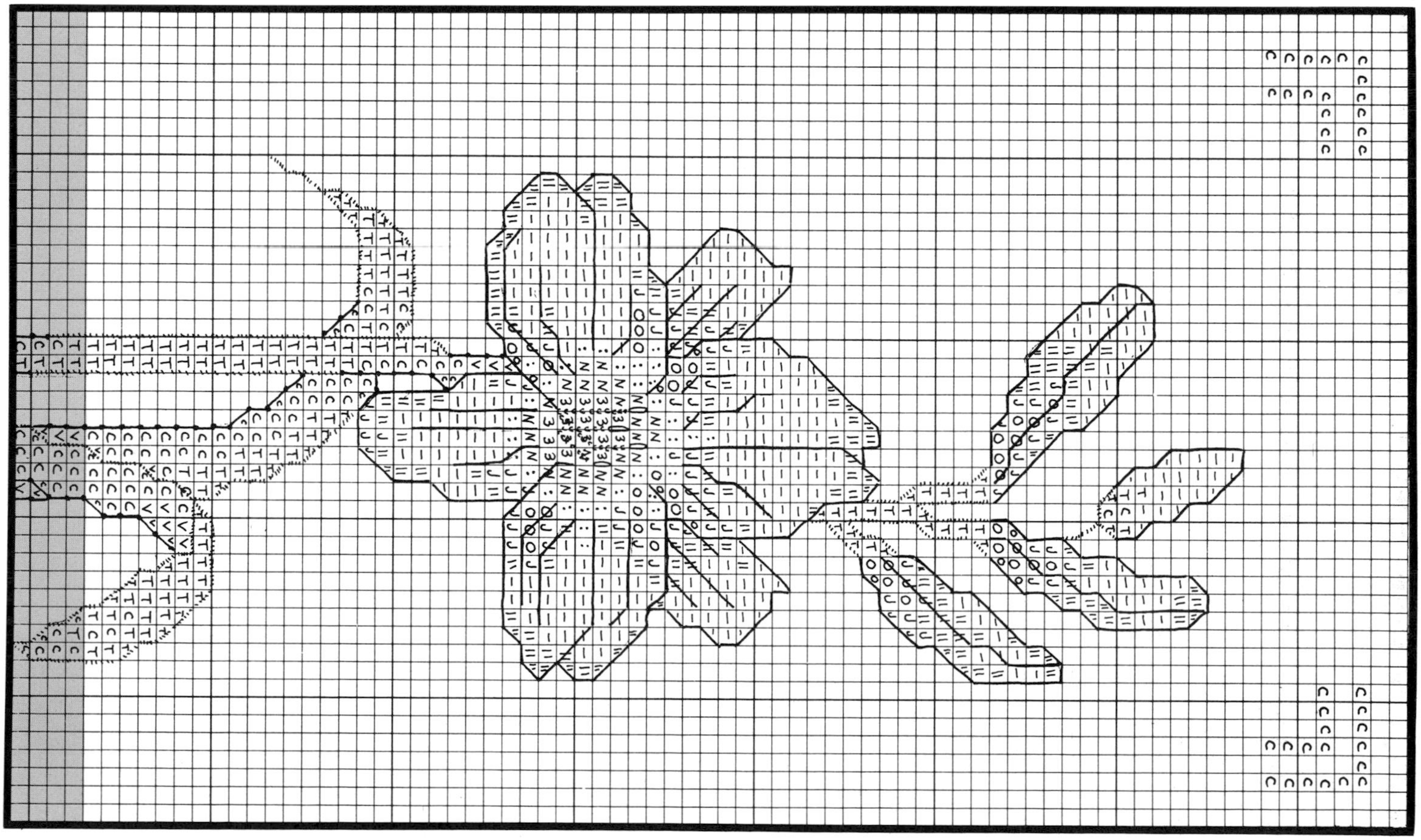

TOP

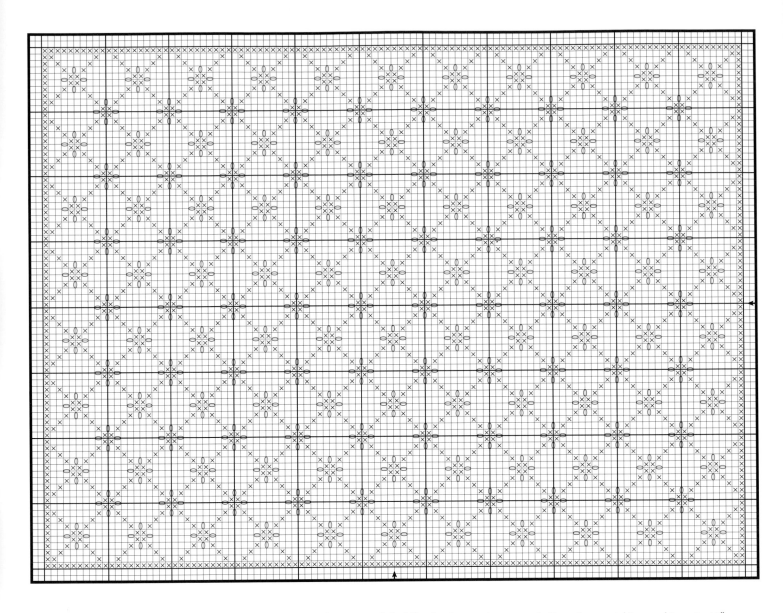

ROSE TRELLIS PLACE MATS

DMC Coats Anchor®

| x | 3347 | 6266 | 267 | yellow-green, med. (eight skeins) |
| LD 899 | 3282 | 38 | | rose, med. (6 skeins) |

Fabric used for models: 14-count pink Aida
Stitch count: 80H x 110W
Approximate design size:
    14-count—5 ¾" x 7 ⅞"
    18-count—4 ⅜" x 6 ⅛"

Instructions: Cross stitch using three strands of floss. Make Lazy Daisy (LD) stitches using two strands 899/3282/38. NOTE: Work design from left to right. DO NOT SKIP AROUND.
Finishing instructions:
NOTE: Yardage listed is for two place mats and napkins.

1. Complete cross stitch following instructions given.
2. Purchase 1 ½ yds. 44/45"-wide complementary floral print fabric of your choice, and matching thread.
3. Cut a 13" x 19" piece of floral print fabric for backing. Cut three strips, each 4" wide x 45" long. Sew the strips together to form one long strip. Fold strip in half lengthwise with wrong sides together, stitch close to raw edge, and press. Then make a pleat every 1 ½", pin, and baste along raw edges.
4. With right sides and raw edges together, stitch pleated ruffle to front, using a ¼" seam allowance.
5. With right sides together, stitch 13" x 19" backing piece to front, making sure pleated trim lays toward center of place mat. Stitch front and back pieces together using a ¼" seam allowance, and leaving an opening for turning. Trim corners, turn, and press. Slip stitch opening closed.

6. To make a matching napkin, cut a 16" square from remaining floral print fabric. Turn raw edges under ½" and press. Turn edges under ½" again, stitch around perimeter of napkin close to folded edge, and press.

Designed by Hope Murphy

LAZY DAISY STITCH

To work Lazy Daisy stitch, bring needle up at 1, and go down at 2 (in the same hole), leaving a loop in the floss. Then bring needle up at 3, pulling up slack in floss loop, and go down at 4 to secure loop.

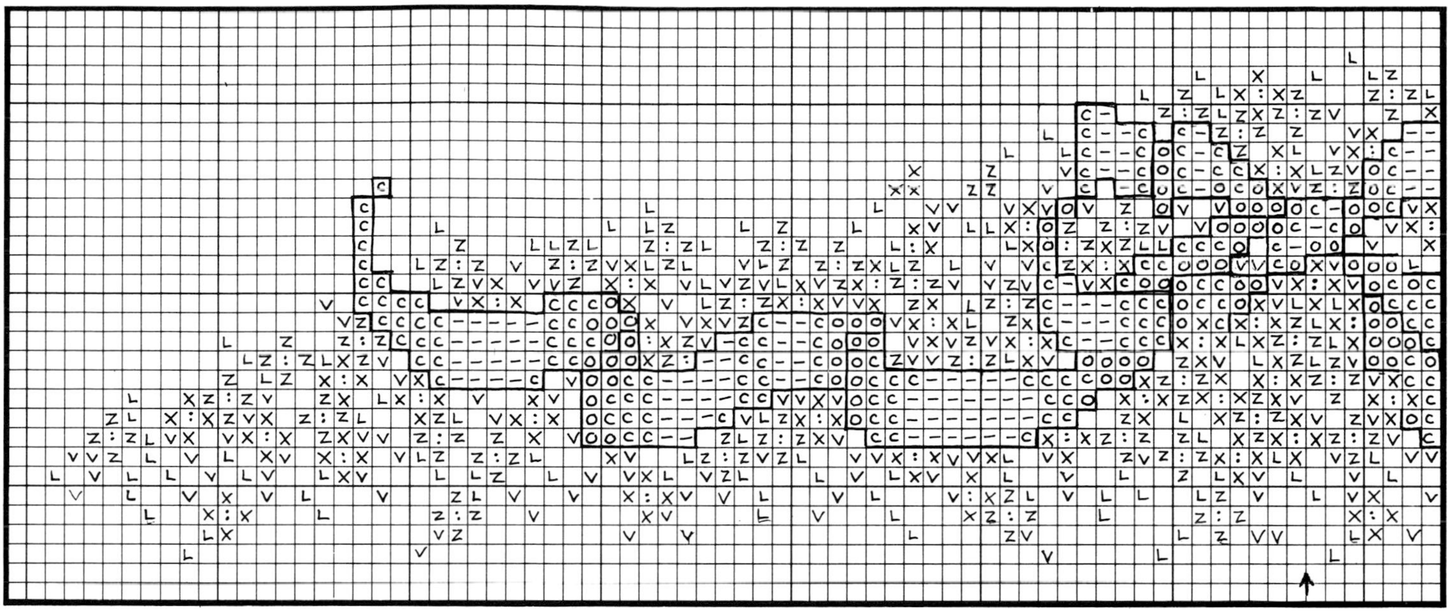

FORGET-ME-NOTS AND RIBBONS PLACE MAT AND NAPKIN

	DMC	Coats	Anchor®	
o	223	3241	895	pink, med.
c	224	3240	894	pink, lt.
-	225	3239	892	pink, vy. lt.
x	3766	—	—	peacock blue, lt.
z	518	—	169	wedgewood, lt.
:	676	2305	887	old gold, lt.
L	3347	6266	267	yellow-green, med.
V	3346	6258	268	hunter
bs	3721	—	—	pink, vy. dk.

Fabric used for model: 14-count ivory Royal Classic place mat and napkin from Charles Craft, Inc.

Stitch count: Place mat —27H x 132W
    Napkin—36H x 36W

Approximate design size:
    Place mat—2" x 9 ⅜"
    Napkin—2 ½" x 2 ½"

Instructions: Cross stitch using three strands of floss. Backstitch using two strands 3721/—/—.

Place mat
Center design 18 squares in from inside edge of fringe at left edge of place mat.

Napkin
Stitch design 18 squares in from inside edge of fringe in one corner, referring to center marks on chart for placement.

Designed by Linda Jary

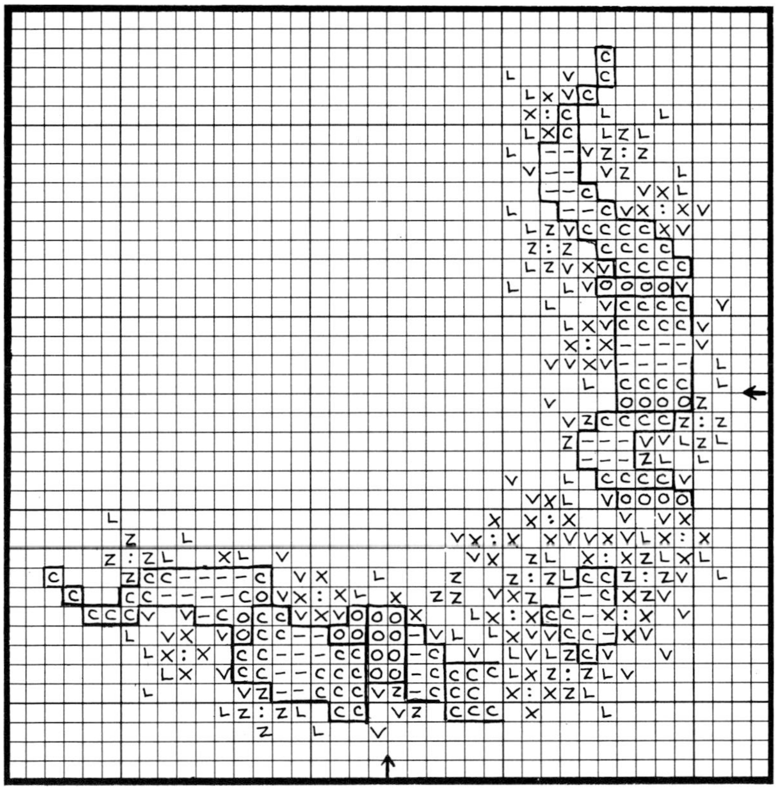

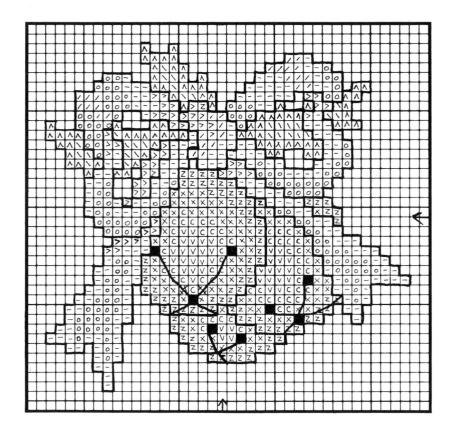

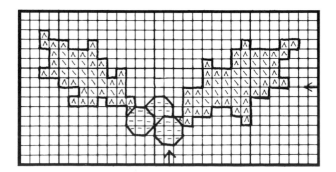

JINGLE BELLS PLACE MAT AND NAPKIN

	DMC	Coats	Anchor®	
z	782	—	308	topaz, med.
x	783	—	307	gold
c	725	2298	305	topaz
V	726	2294	295	topaz, lt.
■	3371	5478	382	black-brown
>	902	3083	897	garnet, vy. dk.
-	815	3000	22	garnet, med.
o	321	3500	47	red
/	351	3011	10	coral
∧	987	6258	244	forest, dk.
\	989	6266	242	forest

Fabric used for model: 27-count ivory Super Linen from Charles Craft, Inc.
Stitch count:
    Place mat—36H x 38W
    Napkin—12H x 27W
Approximate design size:
    Place mat—2 ⅝" x 2 ⅞"
    Napkin—⅞" x 2"

Instructions: Cross stitch over two threads using two strands of floss. Backstitch using one strand of floss unless indicated otherwise. NOTE: Cut fabric to standard size, referring to "General Instructions and Helpful Hints." Place mat: Stitch design 1 ½" in from left side edge and 1 ½" up from lower edge. Napkin: Stitch design 1" in from right side edge and 1 ½" up from lower edge.
Backstitch (bs) instructions:
Place mat
    3371 5478 382 inside bells (two strands), remainder of backstitching (one strand)

Napkin
    3371 5478 382 all backstitching

Designed by Robyn Taylor

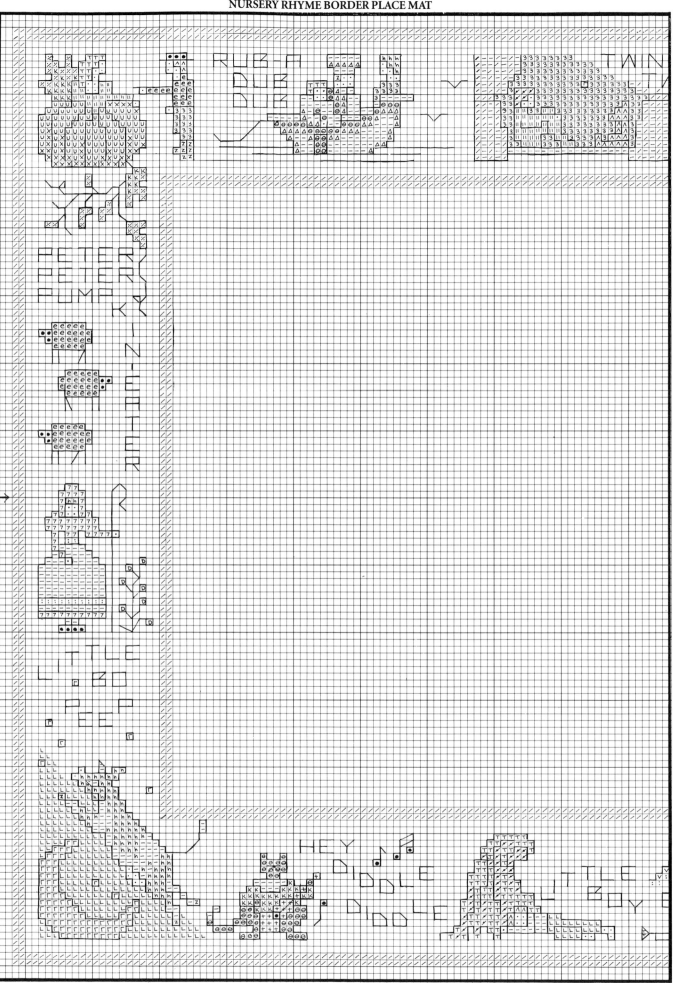

NURSERY RHYME BORDER PLACE MAT

	DMC	Coats	Anchor®	
⁄	321	3500	47	red
N	815	3000	22	garnet, med.
⌐	745	2296	300	yellow, lt. pl.
y	743	2302	302	yellow, med.
∪	742	2303	303	tangerine, lt.
x	741	2314	314	tangerine, med.
‖	828	7053	158	blue, ul. lt.
∟	813	7161	160	blue, lt.
c	826	7180	161	blue, med.
3	825	7181	162	blue, dk.
•	951	3335	933	flesh, vy. lt.
:	955	6030	206	nile green, lt.
V	912	6205	205	emerald, lt.
◢	911	6205	230	emerald, med.
7	3716	—	25	dusty rose, lt.
✎	729	—	874	old gold, med.
T	676	2305	887	old gold, lt.
●	310	8403	403	black
⁒	3348	6266	264	yellow-green, lt.
K	3347	6266	267	yellow-green, med.
∧	436	5943	362	tan
+	435	5371	363	brown, vy. lt.
h	434	5000	370	brown, lt.
z	801	5475	353	coffee, dk.
−	white	1001	01	white
⌐	738	5375	372	tan, vy. lt.
e	ecru	1002	387	ecru
D	210	4303	108	lavender, med.
Δ	762	8510	397	pearl gray, vy. lt.
Θ	415	8510	398	pearl gray
G	922	3336	347	copper, lt.

Fabric used for model: 14-count white Aida
Stitch count: 140H x 216W
Approximate design size:
  14-count—10" x 15 ⅜"
  18-count—7 ⅜" x 12"
  22-count—6 ⅜" x 9 ⅞"

Instructions: Cross stitch using three strands of floss. Backstitch using two strands 310/8403/403. Make French knots for nose on cat and dog using two strands 310/8403/403, wrapping around needle twice. NOTE: Cut fabric 14" x 19". Turn raw edges under ½" and press. Turn edges under ½" again, stitch around perimeter of place mat close to folded edge, and press.

Designed by Linda Jary

THREE LETTER MONOGRAM COLLECTION

Stitch count: 40H x 40W (one complete monogram)

Blue Towels
  DMC Coats Anchor®
  224   3240   894 pink, lt.

Bath towel—10-count waste canvas
Approximate design size: 4" x 6"

Hand towel—18-count waste canvas
Approximate design size: 2 ¼" x 2 ¼"

Instructions: Cross stitch using six strands of floss on 10-count waste canvas. Cross stitch using three strands of floss on 18-count waste canvas.

Rose Towel
  DMC Coats Anchor®
  3325   7976   144 baby blue

Face towel—12-count waste canvas
Approximate design size: 3 ⅜" x 3 ⅜"

Instructions: Cross stitch using four strands of floss.
NOTE: Velour towels may be purchased at most department stores.

Pillowcase
  DMC Coats Anchor®
  210   4302   108 lavender, med.

Pillowcase—14-count waste canvas
Approximate design size: 2 ⅞" x 2 ⅞"

Instructions: Cross stitch using two strands of floss.

Place Mat and Napkin
  DMC Coats Anchor®
  white 1001   01   white

Fabric used for model: 28-count white Super Linen from Charles Craft, Inc.
Approximate design size: 2 ⅞" x 2 ⅞"

Instructions: Cross stitch over two threads using two strands of floss. NOTE: Place mat: Cut fabric 12 ½" x 18". Center monogram on left side 1" in from edge of fabric. When stitching is complete, machine stitch ½" in from edge. Fringe by pulling threads from edges to machine stitching. Napkin: Cut fabric 14" x 14". Stitch monogram 1" in from left side edge and 1" up from lower edge. Fringe by pulling threads from edges to machine stitching. NOTE: On alphabet letters O and P, dotted lines have been added for alphabet letters Q and R.

Designed by Linda Jary

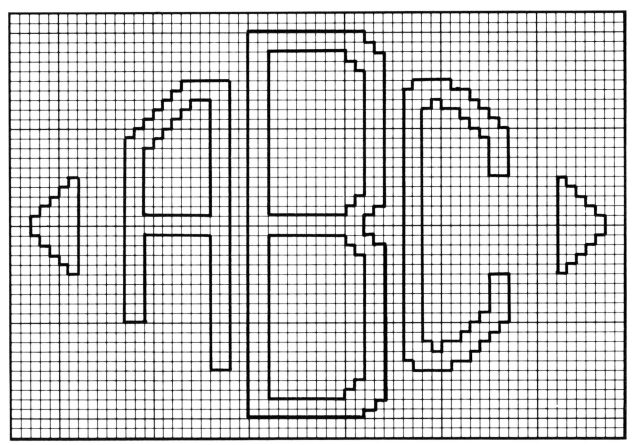

Illustration has been given to show placement of letters.

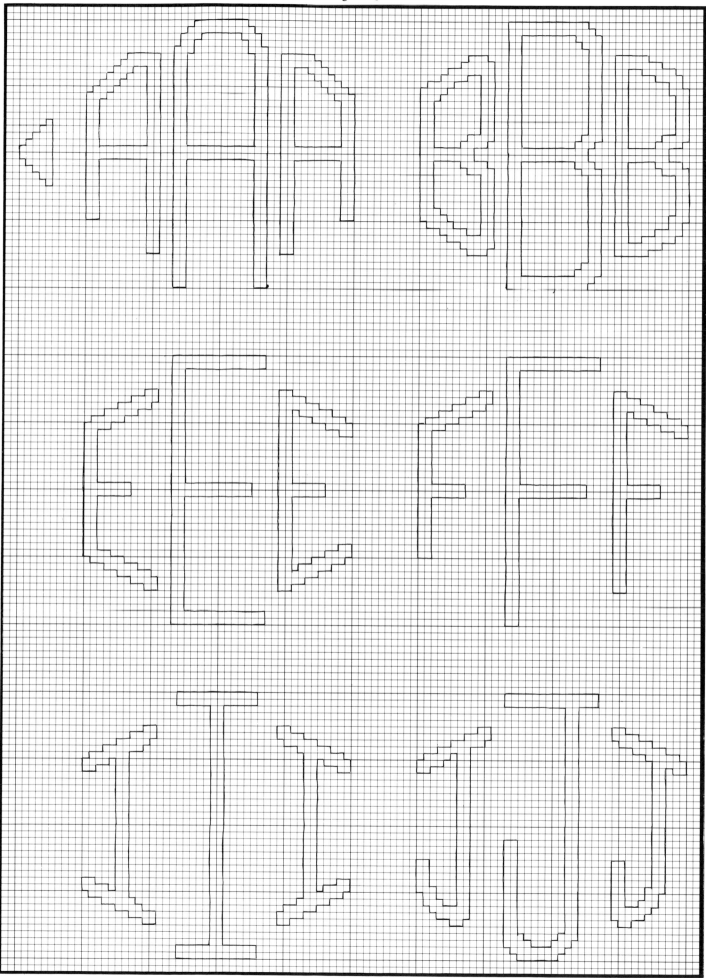

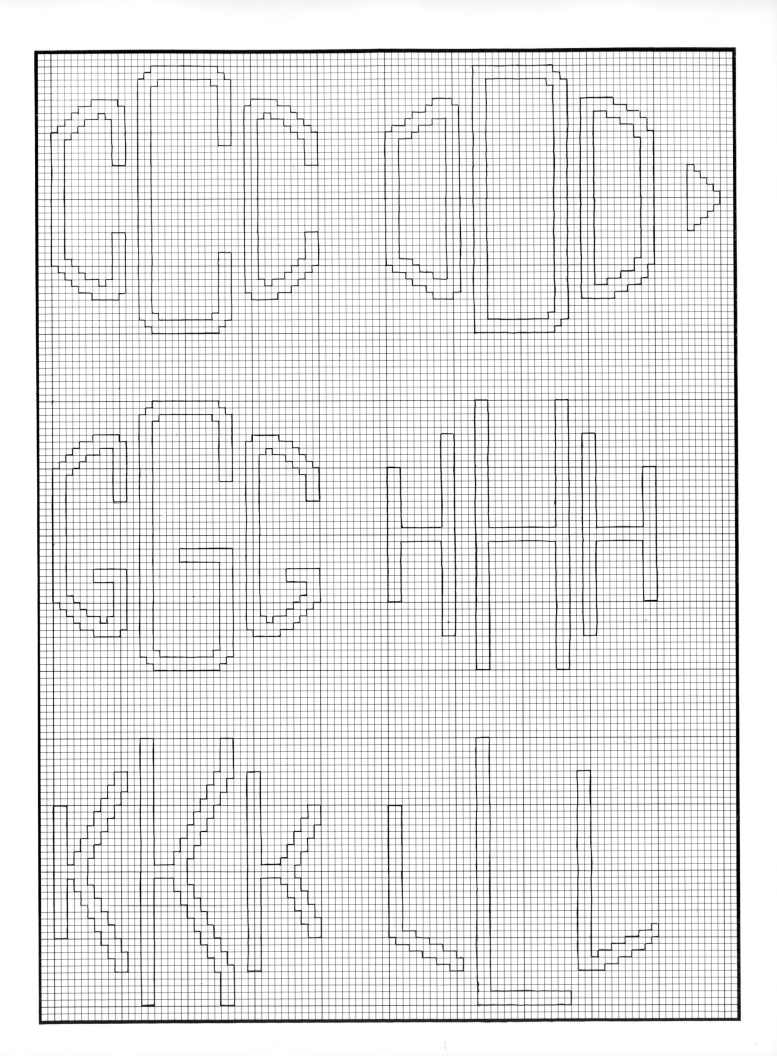

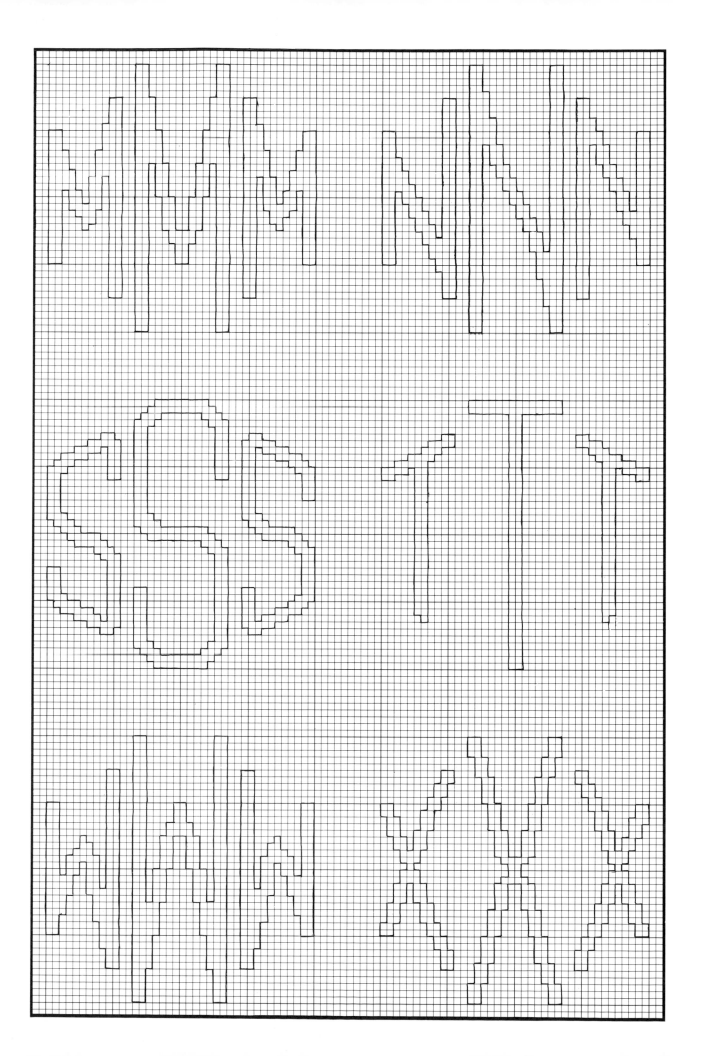

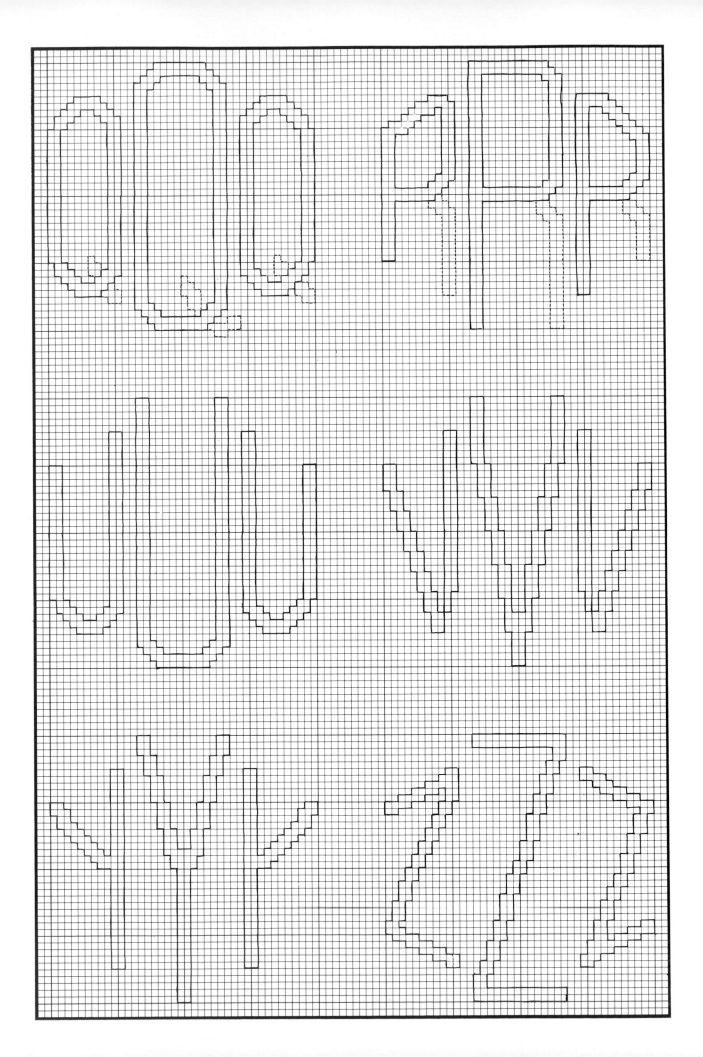

MONOGRAM QUARTET PLACE MATS

DMC Coats Anchor®

■	500	6880	879	blue green, vy. dk.
6	501	6878	878	blue green, dk.
╲	922	3336	347	copper, lt.
⊙	921	—	349	copper
x	931	7051	921	antique blue, med.
=	932	7050	343	antique blue, lt.
o	3752	—	976	antique blue
3	680	—	907	old gold, dk.
V	729	—	874	old gold, med.
╱	676	2305	887	old gold, lt.
N	3740	—	872	antique violet
c	3041	4222	871	antique violet, med.
▬	3042	4221	869	antique violet, lt.
z	3328	3071	10	salmon, med.
‖	3712	—	—	salmon
L	760	3068	893	salmon, lt.
w	3726	—	970	mauve, med. lt.
╱╱	316	3081	969	mauve, med.
I	3727	—	969	mauve
bs	3799	—	236	pewter-gray, vy. dk.

FLORAL MEDALLION MONOGRAM

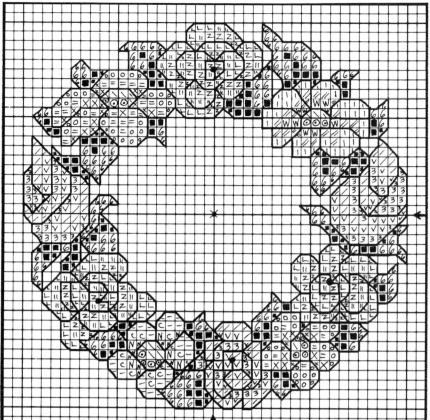

MONOGRAM TRIO

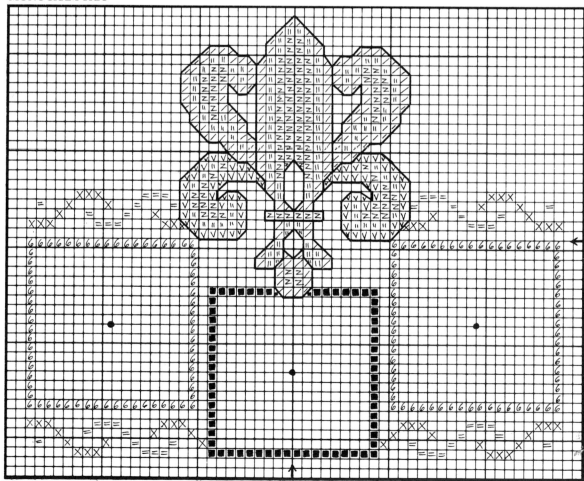

115

Fabric used for model: 26-count Sal-Em cloth pre-finished place mats from Carolina Cross Stitch, Inc.

Tulip Monogram
Stitch count: 33H x 46W
Approximate design size:
 14-count—2 ⅜" x 3 ⅜"
 18-count—1 ¾" x 2 ½"
 26-count—2 ½" x 3 ½"

Floral Shield Monogram
Stitch Count: 42H x 44W
Approximate design size:
 14-count—3" x 3 ¼"
 18-count—2 ⅜" x 2 ½"
 26-count—3 ¼" x 3 ⅜"

Monogram Trio
Stitch count: 46H x 56W
Approximate design size:
 14-count—3 ⅜" x 4"
 18-count—2 ½" 3 ⅛"
 26-count—3 ½" x 4 ⅜"

Floral Medallion Monogram
Stitch count: 40H x 40W
Approximate design size:
 14-count—2 ⅞" x 2 ⅞"
 18-count—2 ¼" x 2 ¼"
 26-count—3 ⅛" x 3 ⅛"

Instructions: Cross stitch over two threads using two strands of floss. Backstitch using one strand of floss unless indicated otherwise. Backstitch Floral Medallion Monogram using 3799/—/236. Floral Medallion Monogram: Make French knots for flower centers using two strands 921/—/349, wrapping around needle twice.
NOTE: Stitch design at top left corner leaving 1" between design and edges of place mat. For placement of initials, match center dots on charts.
Backstitch (bs) instructions:
Tulip Monogram
 3799 — 236 tulip, leaves
 500 6880 879 tulip stems
 729 — 874 border around letters

Floral Shield Monogram
 3799 — 236 flowers
 500 6880 879 border around letters

Monogram Trio
 500 6880 879 emblem

Designed by Cathy Livingston

TULIP MONOGRAM

FLORAL SHIELD MONOGRAM

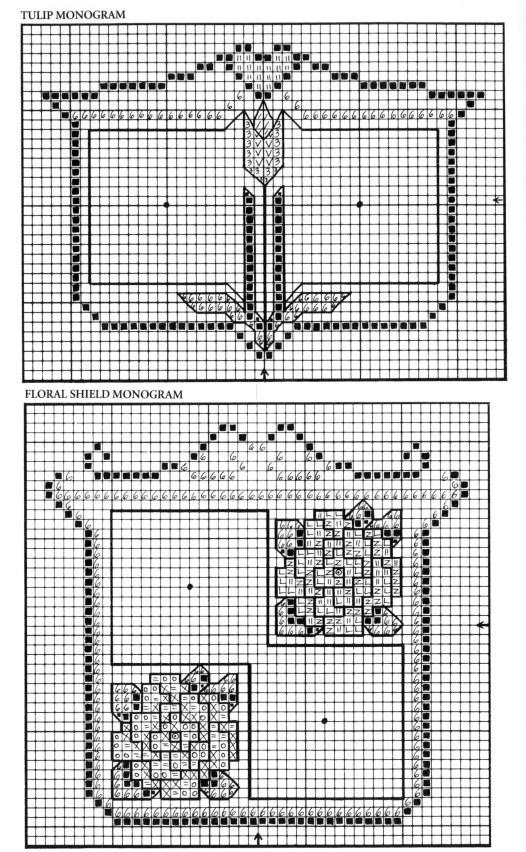

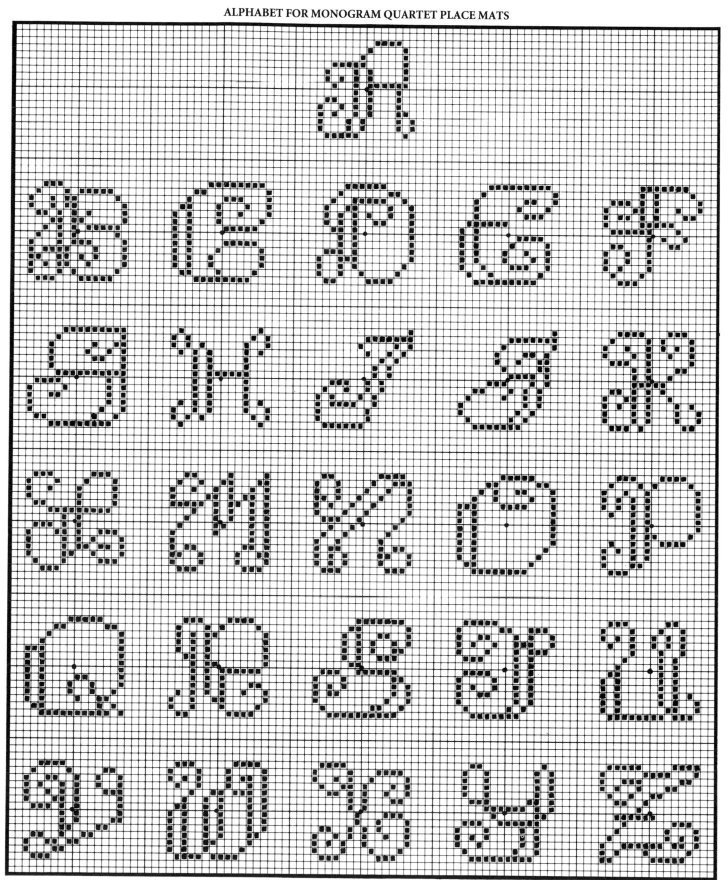

Center dot (•) indicates placement only and is not a stitch symbol.

WILDFLOWER GARDEN TABLE CLOTH CENTER MOTIF

DMC Coats Anchor®

Sym	DMC	Coats	Anchor	Description
▲[	221	3242	897	pink, dk.
	898	5476	360	coffee brown, vy. dk.
◢	934	6270	862	avocado-black
M	936	6269	269	avocado, vy. dk.
✳	937	6268	268	avocado, med.
6	469	6261	268	avocado
x	470	6010	267	avocado, lt.
V	471	6010	266	avocado, vy. lt.
w	3345	6258	269	hunter, dk.
3	3346	6258	268	hunter
>	3347	6266	267	yellow-green, med.
‖	762	8510	397	pearl gray, vy. lt.
•	white	1001	01	white
−[	819	3280	271	baby pink. lt.
	white	1001	01	white
∵[	3078	2292	292	golden yellow, vy. lt.
	white	1001	01	white
∴[	white	1001	01	white
	818	3281	23	baby pink
⊃[	899	3282	38	rose, med.
	white	1001	01	white
ε[	white	1001	01	white
	3350	3004	69	dusty rose, vy. dk.
⊙[	white	1001	01	white
	3354	3003	75	dusty rose, lt.
╱	3078	2292	292	golden yellow, vy. lt.
7[	445	2288	288	lemon, lt.
	472	6253	264	avocado, ul. lt.
▮[	3078	2292	292	golden yellow, vy. lt.
	3013	—	842	khaki, lt.
≠	3325	7976	144	baby blue
2	334	7977	977	baby blue, med.
5	333	—	119	blue violet, dk.
⌐[	341	7005	117	blue violet, lt.
	340	7110	118	blue violet, med.
●	221	3242	897	pink, dk.
₵[	221	3242	897	pink, dk.
	355	2339	5975	terra cotta, dk.
⊖[	356	2338	9575	terra cotta, med.
	355	2339	5975	terra cotta, dk.
=	727	2289	293	topaz, vy. lt.
<	726	2294	295	topaz, lt.
o	725	2298	305	topaz
+[	725	2298	305	topaz
	783	—	307	gold
K[	725	2298	305	topaz
	801	5475	353	coffee, dk.
N	898	5476	360	coffee brown, vy. dk.
9[	783	—	307	gold
	726	2294	295	topaz, lt.
8	783	—	307	gold
∷	743	2302	302	yellow, med.
e	351	3011	10	coral
∥	352	3008	9	coral, lt.
L	353	3006	8	peach, flesh
z	602	3063	63	cranberry, med.
ц	601	3128	57	cranberry, dk.
++	604	3001	66	cranberry, lt.
╲	605	—	60	cranberry, vy. lt.
Я[	554	4104	96	violet, lt.
	553	4097	98	violet, med.

Sym	DMC	Coats	Anchor	Description
X	552	4092	101	violet, dk.
a	3607	—	87	plum, lt.
ᄀ[	3609	_	85	plum, ul. lt.
	3608	—	86	plum, vy. lt.
G[	727	2289	293	topaz, vy. lt.
	3609	—	85	plum, ul. lt.
■	817	2335	19	coral red, vy. dk.
s	349	2335	13	coral, dk.
#[	355	2339	5975	terra cotta, dk.
	830	—	277	olive, dk.
∧[	3078	2292	292	golden yellow, vy. lt.
	3354	3003	75	dusty rose, lt.
y[	3011	—	845	khaki, dk.
	632	—	936	coffee brown, dk.
B[	221	3242	897	pink, dk.
	3011	—	845	khaki, dk.
◣[	221	3242	897	pink, dk.
	938	5477	381	coffee, ul. dk.
T	3011	—	845	khaki, dk.
V	3012	—	844	khaki, med.
E	3013	—	842	khaki, lt.
⟍	356	2338	9575	terra cotta, med.
⅛[	3012	—	844	khaki, med.
	470	6010	267	avocado, lt.
c[	3013	—	842	khaki, lt.
	471	6010	266	avocado, vy. lt.
bs	745	2296	300	yellow, lt. pl.
bs	744	2293	301	yellow, pl.
bs	782	—	308	topaz, med.
bs	318	8511	399	steel gray, lt.
bs	895	6021	246	green, dk.
bs	322	7978	978	navy, vy. dk.

VIOLETS
Corner design for wildflower tablecloth.

DMC Coats Anchor®

Sym	DMC	Coats	Anchor	Description
−	553	4097	98	violet, med.
+	552	4092	101	violet, dk.
z[	white	1001	01	white
	552	4092	101	violet, dk.
x[	3078	2292	292	golden yellow, vy. lt.
	white	1001	01	white
w	3078	2292	292	golden yellow, vy. lt.
6	937	6268	268	avocado, med.
3	469	6261	268	avocado
V	470	6010	267	avocado, lt.
╱	471	6010	266	avocado, vy. lt.

TABLECLOTH
Fabric used for model: 14-count cream Gloria® cloth from Zweigart®(afghan cut: 1 ⅓ yds.)

Oval Motif
Stitch count: 158H x 186W
Approximate design size:
  14-count—11 ¼" 13 ¼"

Violets
Stitch count: 46H X 46W
Approximate design size:
  14-count—3 ¼" x 3 ¼"

Instructions: Cross stitch using three strands of floss. Backstitch using one strand of floss unless indicated otherwise. Straight stitch using one strand of floss unless indicated otherwise. When two colors are bracketed together, use two strands of first color and one strand of second color unless indicated otherwise.
Backstitch (bs) instructions:

Oval Motif
Diagram will assist in location.

1. Yellow Lady Slipper

DMC	Coats	Anchor	Description
3011	—	845	yellow petals coming out from *slipper*
782	—	308	*slipper*
895	6021	246	stem, lower edges of lower two leaves
3346	6258	268	remainder of leaves

2. Blue-Eyed grass

DMC	Coats	Anchor	Description
322	7978	978	flower petals
470	6010	267	stems
469	6261	268	leaves

3. Violet (Purple)

DMC	Coats	Anchor	Description
552	4094	101	flower petals
937	6268	268	leaves and stems

4. Wild Geranium

DMC	Coats	Anchor	Description
3607	—	87	flower petals
3346	6258	268	leaves and stems

5. Violets (Yellow)

DMC	Coats	Anchor	Description
783	—	307	flower petals
937	6268	268	leaves and stems

6. Painted Trillium

DMC	Coats	Anchor	Description
318	8511	399	flower petals
3013	—	842	three small leaves between petals
936	6269	269	large leaves and stem

7. Violet (Blue)

DMC	Coats	Anchor	Description
333	—	119	flower petals
937	6268	268	leaves and stems

8. Violet (Purple)

DMC	Coats	Anchor	Description
552	4092	101	flower petals
937	6268	268	leaves and stems

9. Fire Pink

DMC	Coats	Anchor	Description
725	2298	19	straight stitch lines from flower center (one strand)
817	2335	19	flower petals, including partial bloom
830	—	277	base of each flower, two unopened buds and stems
3346	6258	268	leaves

10. Violet (Blue)

DMC	Coats	Anchor	Description
333	—	119	flower petals
937	6268	268	leaves and stems

CORNER MOTIF (LEFT)

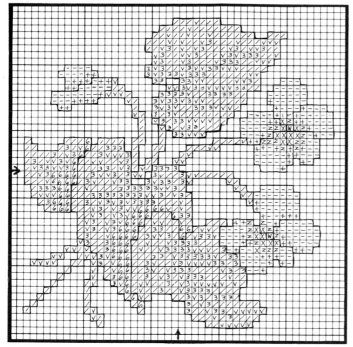

CORNER MOTIF (RIGHT)

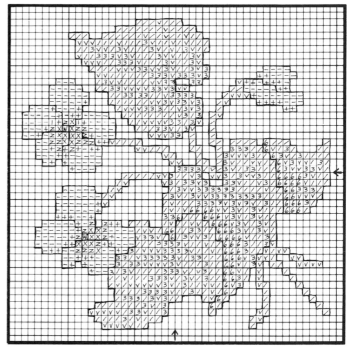

11. Jack-in-the-Pulpit
    (Note: Refer to flower right side up)
    898 5476 360   center of flower
    355 2339 5975 base of flower, stem of
                     flower and leaves of flower
    3013 —   842   top portion of flower
    356 2338 9575 lower edge of two bottom
                     leaves
    3012 —   844   remainder of leaves

12. Wood Sorrel
    899 3282 38   flower petals and buds
    469 6261 268 leaves and stems

13. Eastern Columbine
    351 3011 10   flowers
    [745 2296 300 straight stitch lines from
    744 2293 301 flower tips (one strand
                    each)
    830 —   277   stems
    3346 6258 268 leaves

14. Violet (Yellow)
    783 —   307   flower petals
    937 6268 268 leaves and stems

15. White Trillium
    318 8511 399 flower petals
    725 2298 305 straight stitch lines from
                    flower center (two strands)
    3013 —   842 three small leaves between
                    petals
    936 6269 269 large leaves, and stems

16. Violet (Purple)
    552 4092 101 flower petals
    937 6268 268 leaves and stems

17. Redwood Sorrel
    601 3128 57   flower petals
    3013 —   842 leaves
    3350 3004 69 stems

18. Star Grass
    725 2298 305 flower petals
    470 6010 267 stems
    469 626 268   leaves

19. Violets (Blue)
    333 —   119   flower petals
    937 6268 268 leaves and stems

(continued on page 122)

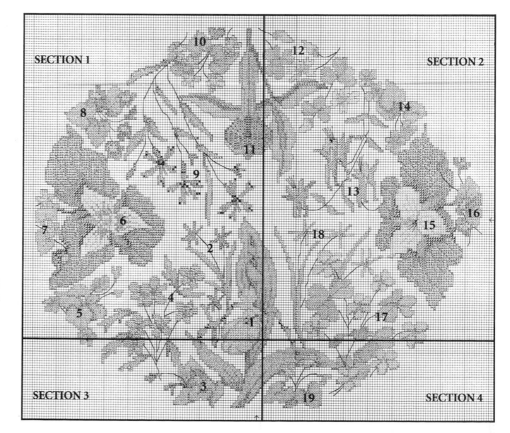

119

Shaded portion indicates overlap from page 120.   **SECTION 3**

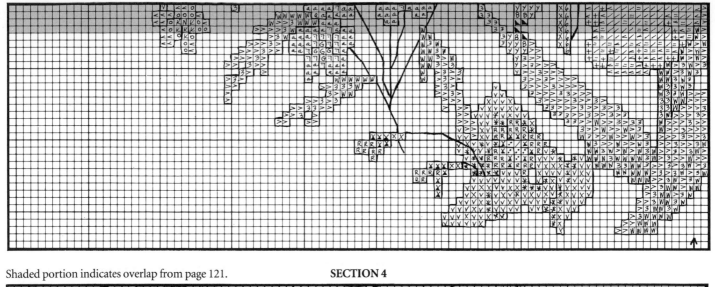

Shaded portion indicates overlap from page 121.   **SECTION 4**

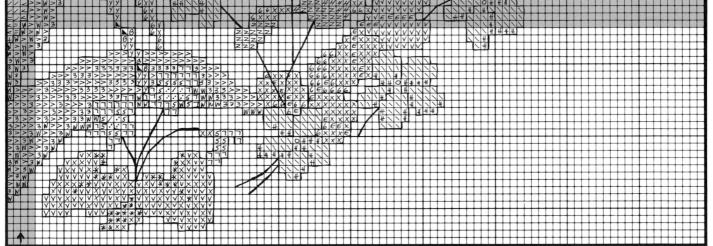

Violets—Corner Motifs

552	4092	101	violet
470	6010	267	stems
469	6261	268	leaves

Finishing Instructions:

1. Purchase 12 yds. ⅛"-wide satin ribbon in complementary color of your choice.

2. Pull two threads from center of each woven border to form a path for the ribbon.

3. Machine stitch 4" from each woven border around perimeter of afghan. Fringe by pulling threads from edges to machine stitching.

4. Using a large tapestry needle, weave ribbon as desired through path made in border.

Designed by Cathy Livingston

RASPBERRIES

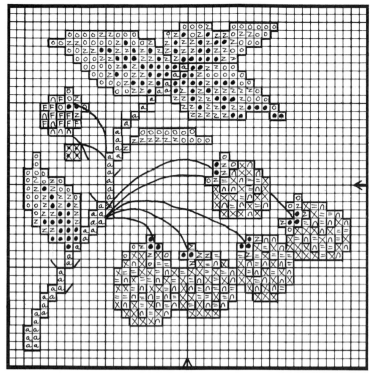

BLUEBERRIES

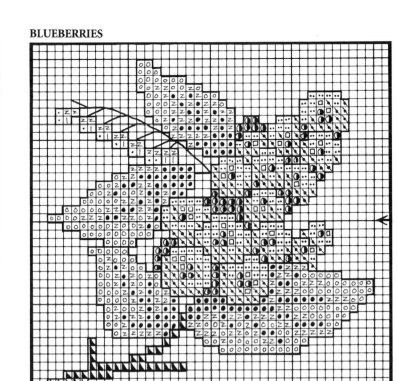

FRUITS AND BERRIES PLACE MATS

DMC Coats Anchor®

9	721	— 324	spice, med.
w[	720	— 326	spice, dk.
	347	3013 13	salmon, dk.
3[	721	— 324	spice, med.
	3328	3071 10	salmon, med.
V[	725	2298 305	topaz
	3712	— —	salmon
-	725	2298 305	topaz
V	761	3068 893	salmon, lt.
++	760	3069 894	salmon
ε	3712	— —	salmon
⊙[	725	2298 305	topaz
	783	— 307	gold
*[	902	3083 897	garnet, vy. dk.
	816	3410 20	garnet
M	816	3410 20	garnet
x[	498	3410 43	red, dk.
	321	3500 47	red
=	321	3500 47	red
•	white	1001 01	white
J	3713	— 968	salmon, ul. lt.
I[	772	6250 253	pine green, lt.
	white	1001 01	white
+	472	6253 264	avocado, ul. lt.
O	471	6010 266	avocado, vy. lt.
◢	720	— 326	spice, dk.
⌐	740	2099 316	tangerine
●	937	6268 268	avocado, med.
▼	890	6021 212	pistachio, ul. dk.
#[	823	7982 150	navy, dk.
	310	8403 403	black
⁄[	823	7982 150	navy, dk.
	312	7979 979	navy, lt.
⌐	367	6018 210	pistachio, dk.

C [	319	6246 246	pistachio, vy. dk.
◣[	830	— 277	olive, dk.
	732	— 281	olive
a[	832	— 907	olive
	732	— 281	olive
∧[	834	— 945	olive, vy. lt.
	734	— 279	olive, lt.
＼	834	— 945	olive, vy. lt.
∥	762	8510 397	pearl gray, vy. lt.
↘[	721	— 324	spice, med.
	834	— 945	olive, vy. lt.
>[	902	3083 897	garnet, vy. dk.
	823	7982 150	navy, dk.
∟[	816	3410 20	garnet
	902	3083 897	garnet, vy. dk.
⫴ [	3722	— 896	pink, dk.
	816	3410 20	garnet
Ɔ[	721	— 324	spice, med.
	725	2298 305	topaz
6[	333	— 119	blue-violet, dk.
	550	4107 102	violet, vy. dk.
<[	3746	— —	blue-violet
	552	4092 101	violet, dk.
∪[	554	4104 96	violet, lt.
	340	7110 118	blue-violet, med.
s[	720	— 326	spice, dk.
	740	2099 316	tangerine
⅃	741	2314 314	tangerine, med.
A	832	— 907	olive
ℓ[	834	— 945	olive, vy. lt.
	3047	2300 956	yellow-beige, lt.
∕	554	4104 96	violet, lt.
K	333	— 119	blue-violet, dk.
≠	3746	— —	blue-violet
∴[	312	7979 979	navy, lt.
	414	8513 235	steel gray, dk.

⌐	340	7110 118	blue-violet, med.
∙	341	7005 117	blue-violet, lt.
R[	834	— 945	olive, vy. lt.
	721	— 324	spice, med.
G[	734	— 279	olive, lt.
	307	2290 289	lemon
4[	472	6253 264	avocado, ul. lt.
	307	2290 289	lemon
⦥	307	2290 289	lemon
∴[	445	2288 288	lemon, lt.
	white	1001 01	white
z	470	6010 267	avocado, lt.
■	3371	5478 382	black-brown
▲	3031	5472 381	mocha, vy. dk.
✕	783	— 307	gold
8[	725	2298 305	topaz
	472	6253 264	avocado, ul. lt.
y	734	— 279	olive, lt.
N[	471	6010 266	avocado, vy. lt.
	472	6253 264	avocado, ul. lt.
∧[	721	— 324	spice, med.
	741	2314 314	tangerine, med.
✎	347	3013 13	salmon, dk.
∩	3328	3071 10	salmon, med.
◖	830	— 277	olive, dk.
▶	498	3410 43	red, dk.
◕	823	7982 150	navy, dk.
◥	311	7980 148	navy, med.
∙∙	312	7979 979	navy, lt.
□	334	7977 977	baby blue, med.
F[	3328	3071 10	salmon, med.
	470	6010 267	avocado, lt.
✕[	471	6010 266	avocado, vy. lt.
	3328	3071 10	salmon, med.

BLACKBERRIES

STRAWBERRIES

LEMONS

CHERRIES

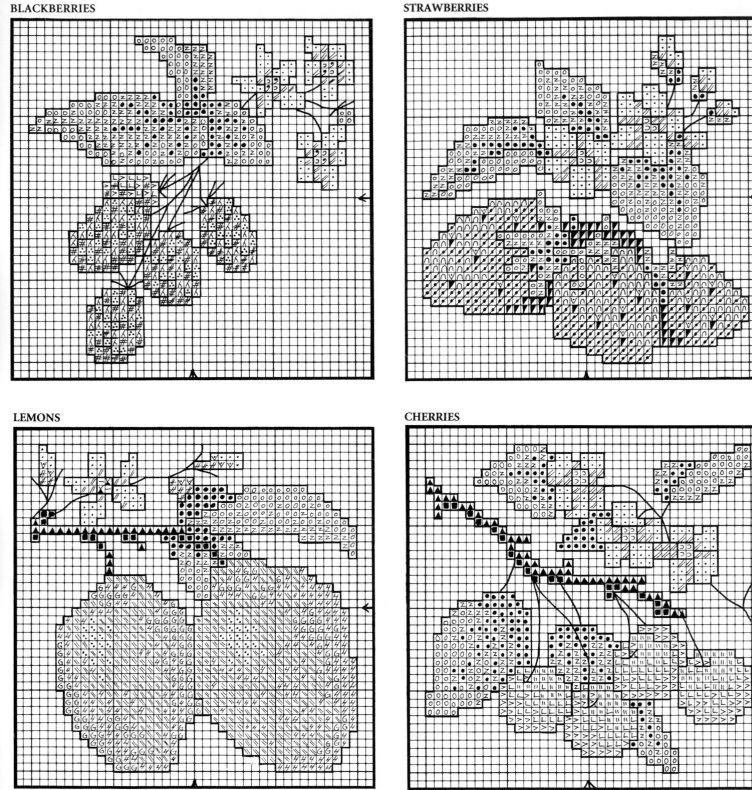

Fabric used for models: 26-count cream or white Sal-Em cloth pre-finished place mats from Carolina Cross Stitch, Inc.; 18-count cream Aida (four corner inserts) tablecloth from Tish and Amy Originals; 14-count cream pre-finished place mats from Charles Craft, Inc.

Stitch count: 40H x 40W

Approximate design size:

    14-count—2 ⅞" x 2 ⅞"

    18-count—2 ¼" x 2 ¼"

    26-count—3" x 3"

    30-count—2 ⅝" x 2 ⅝"

Instructions: Cross stitch over two threads using two strands of floss. Cross stitch using two strands of floss for 14- and 18-count fabrics. Backstitch using one strand of floss.

NOTE: Stitch design at top left corner leaving 1" between design and edges of place mat.

Backstitch (bs) instructions:

    937   6268   268   all stems to flowers, berries, and cherries; tendrils on melons and grapes

    3371   5478   382   remainder of backstitching

Designed by Cathy Livingston

GRAPES

WATERMELON

CANTALOUPE

PLUMS

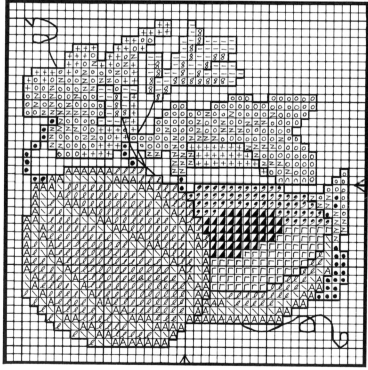

PEARS

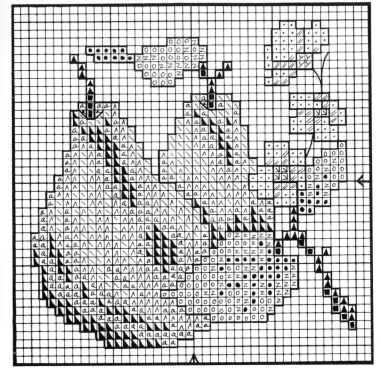

ORANGES

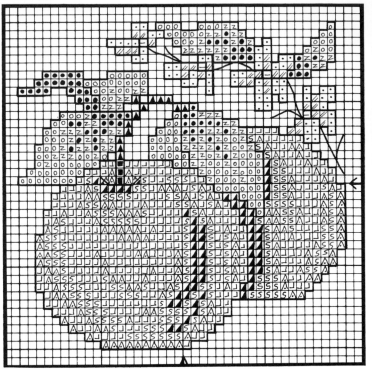

APPLES

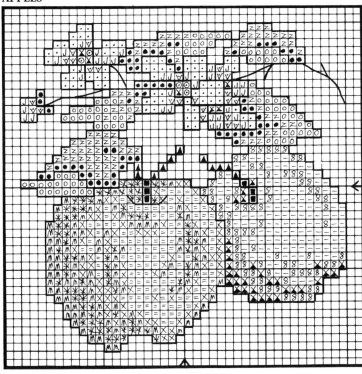

PEACHES

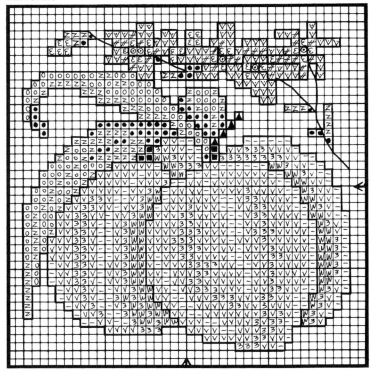

SHOPPERS GUIDE

GARLAND OF FRUITS
Punch Bowl: From a private collection
Fabric: 25-count cream Dublin linen from Zweigart®
Lace: Purchased at a local fabric store

BLUE SILHOUETTE
Dinnerware: Dinnerware on tablecloth: inner plate *Blue Danube* by Blue Danube, and outer plate *Calico* by Staffordshire; dinnerware on place mats: from a private collection
Stemware: Mexican glassware from Pier 1 Imports
Silver: *English Chippendale* by Reed & Barton
Heart-shaped flag box: Nancy Thomas Studio Gallery, Ballard St., Yorktown, VA 23690
Fabrics: 25-count white Lugana® from Zweigart®, and 26-count white Sal-Em cloth pre-finished place mats and napkins with lace from Carolina Cross Stitch, Inc.; table skirt fabric, *Surprise* by Waverly
Lace: Purchased at a local fabric store

PANSY PARADE
Crystal: From a private collection
Fabric: 27-count off white linen from Norden Crafts; table skirt fabric, *Nanchang Mini* by Waverly
Lace: Purchased at a local fabric store

HAPPY BIRTHDAY
Fabric: 14-count white Aida
Lace: Purchased at a local fabric store

GRAPE ARBOR
Crystal, Silver, and Dinnerware: From a private collection
Fabric: 14-count white Louisiana cloth from Wichelt Imports, Inc.

WEDDING BELLS
China: *Noritake Ivory* by Noritake
Crystal: Champagne flutes by Miller-Rogoska
Silver: From a private collection
Cake: Marsh's Bakery, Birmingham, Alabama
Fabric: 28-count white linen from Charles Craft, Inc.
Lace: Purchased at a local fabric store

CELEBRATIONS
China, Crystal, and Silver: From a private collection
Fabric: 26-count white Super Linen from Charles Craft, Inc.
Lace: Purchased at a local fabric store

WILDFLOWER GARDEN
Bedspread and Accessories: From a private collection
Bird Cage: The Ritz Florist, Birmingham, Alabama
Teapot: From a private collection
Fabric: 14-count cream Gloria® cloth from Zweigart®

MAGNOLIA BLOSSOM
Fabric: 26-count white Sal-Em cloth pre-finished table runner from Carolina Cross Stitch, Inc.

GRANDMA HILL'S BOUQUET
China: *Export Blue*
China tea service: From a private collection
Fabric: 26-count white Sal-Em cloth pre-finished table runner from Carolina Cross Stitch, Inc.

BOUNTIFUL HARVEST
Fabric: 26-count cream table runner with fringe from Carolina Cross Stitch, Inc.

PRIMITIVE TABLE RUNNER
Fabric: 14-count parchment Yorkshire Aida from Zweigart®

REINDEER AND RIBBON
China: Rose by Schumann, Bavaria
Silver: From a private collection
Linen napkins: Purchased at a local antique shop
Fabric: 25-count Christmas red Lugana® from Zweigart®
Lace: Purchased at a local fabric store

PARASOL BOUQUET
Doll: From a private collection
Pitcher: From a private collection
Fabric: 28-count periwinkle blue linen from Zweigart®

FOUR FLOWERS ON NAVY
Dinnerware: *Green Majolica* from Pier 1 Imports, and *Blue Peony* by Nikko
Vase: *Export Blue*
Fabric: 28-count navy Jobelan from Wichelt Imports, Inc.

ROSE TRELLIS
Dinnerware and Glassware: From Pier 1 Imports
Fabric: 14-count pink Aida

NURSERY RHYME BORDER
Dinnerware: From Pier 1 Imports
Baby Utensils: *Tommee Tippee* from Baby Superstore
Fabric: 14-count white Aida

JINGLE BELLS
China: *Holiday* by Lenox
Silver: From a private collection
Crystal: Cranberry stemware from a local antique shop
Brass Candlesticks and Star Ornaments: The Ritz Florist,
       Birmingham, Alabama
Fabric: 27-count ivory Super Linen from Charles Craft, Inc.

FORGET-ME-NOTS AND RIBBONS
Dinnerware: *Pink Spongeware* plates, and antique *Historic America* plates by Johnson Brothers, from
       private collections
Silverware: by Wallace
Fabric: 14-count ivory Royal Classic place mat and napkin
       from Charles Craft, Inc.

THREE LETTER MONOGRAM COLLECTION
Dinnerware: *Metropolis Black* by Sasaki
Silverware: From a private collection
Fabrics: 28-count white Super Linen from Charles Craft, Inc.
Towels and pillowcase: Purchased at a local department store

MONOGRAM QUARTET
Crystal, Silver, and Cranberry Glassware: From a private collection

White Dinnerware: From Pier 1 Imports
Fabric: 26-count Sal-Em cloth pre-finished place mats from
       Carolina Cross Stitch, Inc.

FRUITS AND BERRIES
China and Silver: From a private collection
Fabrics: 26-count cream or white Sal-Em cloth pre-finished
       place mats from Carolina Cross Stitch, Inc.; 18-count
       cream Aida (four corner inserts) tablecloth from Tish
       and Amy Originals; 14-count cream pre-finished
       place mats from Charles Craft, Inc.

Special thanks to The Birmingham Botanical Gardens, The Caroline House, Dr. and Mrs. James Crenshaw, Mr. and Mrs. Charles Hill, Mr. and Mrs. Wayne Hoffman, Mr. and Mrs. Robert Holmes, Mr. and Mrs. Jack James, Mr. and Mrs. William H. MacMillan, Mr. and Mrs. Walter Monroe, Mrs. Glenda Parker, Mr. and Mrs. Charles H. Peay, Jr., Mr. and Mrs. John Roberts, Birmingham, Alabama, for providing the photography locations in this book.

Items not listed in "Shoppers Guide" are either commonly available, antiques, or are from private collections.

CREDITS

Editors
   Barbara Cockerham
   Phyllis Hoffman
Associate Editor
   Diane Kennedy
Production Vice President
   Wayne Hoffman
Creative Director
   Mac Jamieson
Art Director
   Yukie McLean
Associate Production Manager
   Perry James
Editorial Assistants
   Donna Rush
   Carol Odom
Computer Graphics Designers
   Scott Begley
   Janet Roberts
   Keith Lawler
Staff Artist
   Casey Day

Photography Stylist
   Tracey MacMillan
Studio Assistant
   Clay Wortham

Designers
   Cathy Livingston   Linda Jary
   Dot Young   Robyn Taylor
   Hope Murphy
Stitchers
   Katherine Bousack   Nora Bowen
   Denise Brown   Julie Casey
   Bettye Dwyer   Melissa Gachet
   Patsy Gilley   Shelia Gray
   Pam Hatcher   Elane Jones
   Joan Lanier   Felicia McEachin
   Kara Miller   Rebecca Mitchell
   Emily Neel   Ella Robinson
   Catherine Scott   Karen Taylor
   Tammy Webber
Custom Finishing
   Lurline Rutland